# SECURING INDIA'S BORDERS

## CHALLENGES AND POLICY OPTIONS

# SECURING INDIA'S BORDERS

## CHALLENGES AND POLICY OPTIONS

GAUTAM DAS

Centre for Land Warfare Studies

PENTAGON PRESS

The Centre for Land Warfare Studies (CLAWS), New Delhi, is an autonomous think tank dealing with contemporary issue of national activity and conceptual aspects of land warfare, including conventional and sub-conventional conflicts and terrorism. CLAWS conducts research that is futuristic in outlook and policy-oriented in approach.

Centre for Land Warfare Studies
RPSO Complex, Parade Road, Delhi Cantt, New Delhi-110010
Phone: 011-25691308 • Fax: 011-25692347
email: landwarfare@gmail.com • website: www.claws.in

*Securing India's Borders: Challenges and Policy Options* / Gautam Das

ISBN 978-81-8274-532-2

First Published in 2011
Reprinted 2012



The views expressed are the personal views of the author and do not necessarily represent the views of CLAWS.

*Published by*

PENTAGON PRESS
206, Peacock Lane, Shahpur Jat,
New Delhi-110049
Phones: 011-64706243, 26491568
Telefax: 011-26490600
email: rajan@pentagonpress.in
website: www.pentagon-press.com

*Printed at*
Avantika Printers Pvt. Ltd.

# Contents

## Part II: FORCES

# Foreword

Due to the proclivity of India's neighbours to exploit the country's nation-building difficulties, India's internal security challenges are inextricably linked with border management. This is so because Indian insurgent groups have for long been provided shelter across the nation's borders by inimical neighbours. The challenge of coping with long-standing territorial and boundary disputes with China and Pakistan, combined with porous borders along some of the most difficult terrain in the world, has made effective and efficient border management a national priority. However, due to the lack of understanding of such military issues among the decision-making elite, India's borders continue to be manned by a large number of military, para-military and police forces, each with its own ethos and reporting to a different central ministry at New Delhi, with almost no real coordination in managing the borders.

External threats to India's territorial integrity are not the only complex border management issue that national security decision makers need to deal with. India's rate of growth has far outpaced that of most of its neighbours, which has generated peculiar problems like mass migration into India. The demographic map of Lower Assam has been completely re-drawn by illegal migration from Bangladesh over several decades. Other threats and challenges have also emerged. The border security scenario is marked by increased cross-border terrorism; infiltration and ex-filtration of armed militants; emergence of non-state actors; nexus between narcotics traffickers and arms smugglers; left-wing extremism; separatist movements aided and abetted by external powers; and the establishment of *madrasas*, some of which are potential security hazards.

Ideally, border management should be the responsibility of the Ministry of Home Affairs during peacetime. However, the active nature of the Line of Control (LoC) and the need to maintain troops close to the Line of Actual Control (LAC) in a state of readiness for operations in high altitude areas, have compelled the army to permanently deploy large forces for this task.

While the BSF should be responsible for all settled borders, the responsibility for unsettled and disputed borders, such as the LoC in J&K and the LAC on the Indo-Tibetan border, should be that of the Indian Army. The principle of 'single point control' must be followed if the borders are to be effectively managed. Divided responsibilities never result in effective control. Despite sharing the responsibility with several para-military and police forces, the army's commitment for border management amounts to six divisions along the LAC, the LoC and the Actual Ground Position Line (AGPL) in J&K and five divisions along the LAC and the Myanmar border in the eastern sector.

This is a massive commitment that is costly in terms of manpower as well as funds, as the deployment areas are mostly in high altitude terrain, and needs to be reduced gradually. The real payoff of a rapprochement with the Chinese would be the possibility of reducing the army's deployment on the LAC. To some extent, the advances in surveillance technology, particularly satellite and aerial imagery, can help to maintain a constant vigil along the LAC and make it possible to reduce physical deployment as and when modern surveillance assets can be provided on a regular basis to the formations deployed forward. Similarly, the availability of a larger number of helicopter units will enhance the quality of aerial surveillance and the ability to move troops to quickly occupy defensive positions when necessary. However, these are both costly ventures and need to be viewed in the overall context of the availability of funds for modernisation. Also, rapid deployment forces will need to be kept ready for unforeseen eventualities.

The deployment patterns of CPOs are marked by ad hoc decisions and knee-jerk reactions to emerging threats and challenges, rather than a cohesive long-term approach that maximises the strength of each organisation. According to Dr GP Bhatnagar, a practitioner and a perceptive observer of the border management scene, the major lacunae that exist in the process include the deployment of multiple forces in the same area of operations and the lack of well articulated doctrinal concepts. He has also written that border management is designed for a 'fire fighting' approach rather than a 'fire prevention' or pro-active approach; it is based on a strategy of 'reaction and retaliation' rather than on a holistic response to the prevailing environment, resulting in stress and decision-making problems at the functional level; it leads to wastage of energy and efforts; and the lack of coordination and synergy between the security management organisations is harmful to the national interest.

A task force on Border Management was constituted by the Group of Ministers (GoM) to review the major issues pertaining to the management of national security after the Kargil conflict. It was led by Madhav Godbole, a former Home Secretary, and had made several far-reaching recommendations. It had recommended that the CRPF should be designated as the primary national level counter-insurgency force. This would enable the other CPMFs like BSF and ITBP to return to their primary role of better border management. It had also recommended that all para-military forces managing unsettled borders should operate directly under the control of the army and that there should be lateral induction from the army to the para-military forces so as to enhance their operational effectiveness. Besides these recommendations, it had suggested several perceptive measures for better inter-agency and inter-ministerial intelligence coordination.

The task force had studied the steps needed to improve border management and had suggested measures for appropriate force structures and procedures to deal with the entry of narcotics, illegal migrants, terrorists and small arms. It had also examined measures to establish closer linkages with the border population to protect them from subversive propaganda, to prevent unauthorised settlements and to initiate special developmental programmes. The recommendations of the task force were accepted by the GoM and are being implemented in phases. While some action has been taken, clearly much more needs to be done to make border management more effective. It is time the Godbole task force report on border management is de-classified and put in the public domain.

In order to address the gaps in understanding the major issues involved in better border management among members of the security policy and strategic communities, CLAWS had requested Col Gautam Das (Retd) to undertake a comprehensive study of the challenges and suggest remedial measures. This excellent monograph is the product of his fine efforts. Col Das has not only personally served on most of India's borders, but has also brought to bear the full force of his analytical skills and able scholarship as a well-known author to dispassionately analyse the complex and varied border management challenges confronting the nation. His recommendations for improved border management are extremely practicable and sound. I am sure this short book will go a long way towards enhancing understanding of the complexities of border management.

**Gurmeet Kanwal**
Director, CLAWS

# Abbreviations

| | |
|---|---|
| 2IC | Second in Command |
| AB | Airborne |
| AFSPA | Armed Forces (Special Powers) Act, 1958 |
| AGPL | Actual Ground Position Line |
| ANE's | Anti-national Elements |
| AR | Assam Rifles |
| BDR | Bangladesh Rifles |
| BFSR | Battlefield Surveillance Radar |
| BGF | Border Guarding Force |
| BOP | Border Outpost |
| BPF | Border Police Force |
| BSF | Border Security Force |
| C4ISR | Command, Control, Communications, Computers, Intelligence, Surveillance & Reconnaissance |
| CCS | Cabinet Committee on Security |
| CENTO | Central Treaty Organisation |
| CFL | Cease-fire Line |
| CISF | Central Industrial Security force |
| CPI (Maoist) | Communist Party of India (Maoist) |
| CPF | Central Police Force |
| CPMF | Central Para-Military Force |
| CRPF | Central Reserve Police Force |
| CDS | Chief of Defence Staff |

| | |
|---|---|
| CAS | Close Air Support |
| CG | Coast Guard |
| CHT | Chittagong Hill Tracts |
| CO | Commanding Officer |
| CoBRA | Combat Battalion for Resolute Action |
| COIN | Counter-insurgency |
| CSPF | Coastal Security Police Force |
| DBO | Daulat Beg Oldi |
| DCB | Ditch-cum-bund |
| DIG | Deputy Inspector General |
| DSC | Defence Security Corps |
| Dy SP | Deputy Superintendent of Police |
| EFR | Eastern Frontier Rifles |
| EMP | Electro-magnetic Pulse |
| FATA | Federally Administered Tribal Areas |
| FF | Frontier Force |
| GOC-in-C | General Officer Commanding-in-Chief |
| GoM | Group of Ministers |
| GR | Gorkha Rifles |
| HE | High Explosive |
| HQ | Headquarters |
| IAF | Indian Air Force |
| IG | Inspector General |
| IMBL | International Maritime Boundary Line |
| IPS | Indian Police Service |
| ITBP | Indo-Tibetan Border Police |
| IS Duties | Internal Security Duties |
| IB | International Boundary |
| IRLA | Individual Running Ledger Account |
| ISI | Inter-Services Intelligence |

| | |
|---|---|
| J&K | Jammu & Kashmir |
| JCO | Junior Commissioned Officer |
| JeM | Jaish-e-Mohammed |
| JBWG | Joint Boundary Working Group |
| JWG | Joint Working Group |
| KRC | Kargil Review Committee |
| LIA | Lead Intelligence Agency |
| LOB | Left Out of Battle |
| LeT | Lashkar-e-Tayyeba |
| LMG | Light Machine Gun |
| LAC | Line of Actual Control |
| LIC | Low-intensity Conflict |
| LoC | Line of Control |
| LICO | Low Intensity Conflict Operations |
| MMG | Medium Machine Gun |
| MMRCA | Medium Multi-role Combat Aircraft |
| MoD | Ministry of Defence |
| MHA | Ministry of Home Affairs |
| NCC | National Cadet Corps |
| NATO | North Atlantic Treaty Organisation |
| NDMF | National Disaster Management Force |
| NGW | New Generation Warfare |
| NFU | No First Use |
| NSCN (IM) | National Socialist Council of Nagaland (Isaac-Muivah group) |
| NWFP | North-West Frontier Province |
| NBC | Nuclear, Biological and Chemical |
| OP | Observation Post |
| ORBAT | Order of Battle |
| QM | Quarter-Master |

| | |
|---|---|
| PAO (OR) | Pay and Accounts Office (Other Ranks) |
| PATA | Provincially Administered Tribal Areas |
| PBOR | Personnel Below Officer Rank |
| POK | Pakistan-Occupied Kashmir |
| PAP | People's Armed Police |
| PRC | People's Republic of China |
| RAF | Rapid Action Force |
| RR | Rashtriya Rifles |
| SSB | Sashastra Seema Bal |
| SFF | Special Frontier Force |
| SSM | Surface-to-Surface Missile |
| TNW | Tactical Nuclear Weapon |
| TF | Task Force |
| TTP | Tehrik-e-Taliban Pakistan |
| TA | Territorial Army |
| TAVR | Territorial Army Volunteer Reserve |
| TAR | Tibet Autonomous Region |
| TMD | Tibet Military District |
| UG | Underground |
| ULFA | United Liberation Front of Asom |
| USAF | United States Air Force |
| USI | United Service Institution of India |
| USMC | United States Marine Corps |
| VA | Vulnerable Areas |
| VC | Victoria Cross |
| VP | Vulnerable Points |
| VTMS | Vessel Traffic Management System |

# CHAPTER 1

# Introduction

The security scenario in India has become more difficult and complex after 2009. The Pakistan-based Islamic fundamentalist cross-border and sea-borne threat to India has grown, even as the internal security situation in Pakistan itself has deteriorated. The arrest in the United States (US) of the Pakistan-born American citizen David Headley and his interrogation by the US Federal Bureau of Investigation (FBI) has confirmed a degree of complicity by Pakistan's spy agency, the Directorate of Inter-Services Intelligence (ISI). Pakistan's policy of so-called 'strategic defiance'[1] towards India and its current military operational policy, a continuum of actions for both cold peace and hot war, which can be called its "New Generation Warfare" philosophy, now needs to be seriously taken into account. China and Bangladesh are not benign neighbours either. The Chinese strategic studies institutes and the armed forces of the People's Republic of China (PRC) have been publishing studies and articles that talk of the PRC's need to undermine the hold of India's central government in India's peripheral regions. The open border with Nepal, once a benign alignment, now poses existing and potential problems related to India's internal security. Much of India's extensive land borders and a large segment of the Indian coastline have become 'live' borders.

The nation and the government expect the armed forces to maintain the territorial integrity of the country, couched in general layman's language as 'defending the borders'. Therefore, border defence planning for war or near-war conditions, and border management in peace-time, are important parts of India's national security and defence measures. As an integral element of overall national security, and a vital necessity for the maintenance of internal security, these have become more important than ever before.

This study re-assesses India's defence policies with regard to safeguarding its territorial integrity, and reviews its border security policies that deal with the physical securing of its borders. It is mainly but not wholly confined to the land borders, and the scrutiny of arrangements for the maritime borders and the recommendations are of a general nature.

The threat scenarios for India's borders are examined in order to form a basis for re-examination and re-assessment of India's border defence policies and border security arrangements. The two most worrisome borders, the Indo-Pakistan border and the Sino-Indian border, each have a history which has dictated the present defence policies and the day-to-day security arrangements for each. These two borders are, therefore, examined separately. Today's less-threatened borders—the Indo-Bangladesh, the Indo-Myanmar, the Indo-Nepal, and the Indo-Bhutan border—each have some unique features and pose specific problems, which impinge on both border security and internal security. Each of these, therefore, require a separate policy and practice, wherein both border and related internal security issues are simultaneously and holistically addressed. India's long maritime boundary, starting from the partly non-peninsular states of West Bengal and Gujarat, and extending along the peninsular Indian coast where the Indian landmass juts into the Indian Ocean, is a sizable security concern. The island archipelago territories in both the Bay of Bengal and in the Arabian Sea add to the length of the Indian coastline that needs security. All these need periodic re-assessment.

The last review of India's methods of safeguarding its territorial integrity through a border security mechanism was in 1999, following the 1999 Kargil intrusions by the Pakistan Army and the ensuing border conflict. However, that review stopped short of reviewing the actual defence or 'war-fighting' policy for the borders, since it was primarily concerned with fact-finding. A committee headed by K Subrahmanyam, commonly known as the Kargil Review Committee (KRC), was appointed by the Government of India in July 1999. It was tasked with reviewing the events leading up to the Pakistani aggression in the Kargil District of Jammu & Kashmir (J&K) and to recommend such measures as were considered necessary to safeguard national security against such armed intrusions. The KRC Report was submitted on 15 December 1999 and brought to light several grave deficiencies in India's security management system, particularly in the areas of intelligence, border management and defence management. Following the submission of the KRC Report, the Government set up a Group of Ministers (GoM) on 17 April

2000 to review the national security system in its entirety and, in particular, to consider the recommendations of the KRC and formulate specific proposals for implementation.

The GoM appointed four Task Forces (TFs) to facilitate its work, one each on Intelligence Apparatus, Internal Security, Border Management, and Management of Defence. The TFs took into account not only the KRC observations but also those made by several other committees, and also interacted with the concerned ministries. The TF on Border Management was headed by Dr Madhav Godbole. The TF on Management of Defence actually only reviewed the higher defence management apparatus of the Government of India. It did not address issues such as the war-fighting doctrine to be employed. Thus, it did not consider, for example, whether there should be a 'trip-wire' form of border defence posture allied to a counter-penetration force and/or a related cross-border counter-attack strategy. Nor did it consider whether a 'no loss of territory' political direction dictated a necessity for 'second-line' border defence fighting formations. But some of these issues inherently form a part of whatever policies of border defence and border security are to be adopted. The relevant TFs not having debated these issues meant that these very basic considerations of any territorial defence policy remained unaddressed. Thus, some element of 'status quo-ism' or purely reactive historic evolution remains in India's existing border defence policies and border security mechanisms. With these gaps remaining in the substantive coverage of border defence policy, the TFs submitted their reports.

After considering the reports of the various TFs, the GoM finalised its own report and submitted it to the Government in February 2001. The report was considered by the Cabinet Committee on Security (CCS), which, in May 2001, approved the GoM Report and recommendations, except those pertaining to the proposed institution of the Chief of Defence Staff (CDS), on which it was decided that Government would take a view after consulting various political parties. It was decided by the CCS that there should be nodal ministries for the submission of Action Taken Reports on the recommendations contained in different chapters of the Report. The Nodal Ministry appointed for border management was to be the Ministry of Home Affairs (MHA).[2]

Though the GoM Report was accepted by the Government in May 2001, not all of the 130 actionable recommendations which impact on border management had been implemented till December 2008.[3] For example, the recommended lateral transfer of defence personnel of a certain age into Central Para-Military Forces (CPMFs), including the Border Guarding Forces (BGFs), remains both contentious and apparently intractable.[4] In addition, some of the underlying factors to the recommendations have themselves undergone significant changes for the worse in the ensuing decade from July 1999 to 2009. This, in itself, necessitates a re-look at the subject.

A reality under today's conditions is the necessarily high cost of maintaining a professional long-service army with life-long pensionary benefits. Ways to reduce this cost burden, while still effectively maintaining India's territorial integrity, are exercising the minds of defence planners. One possible part-solution which has been under discussion within the Ministry of Defence (MoD) is the employment of part-time citizen-soldiers, with the necessary motivation and appropriate levels of training, but with lesser benefits from the public exchequer than full-time long-service professionals. Such part-time soldiers already existing are the officers and men of the Territorial Army (TA), but their given role and actual employment, is still based on the security conditions prevailing a half-century ago. Another part-solution could be the re-creation of an Army Reserve, which has progressively disappeared in Indian defence planning[5] after the 1977 changes in the enlistment and service terms of the Army's soldiers.[6] If and when such forces are re-created, they would need to be used in conjunction with the regular forces, as a formal part of an integrated border defence plan.

This monograph takes into account the historical evolution of the existing system. The security of Indian land and maritime borders and of the border zone is examined both under normal or 'peacetime' conditions, and in 'near war' and wartime scenarios. That India's long coastline is not free from hostile attack either has been made amply clear in the recent sea-borne commando-type Islamic *jihadi* assault on Mumbai on 26 November 2008, which was launched from the Pakistani port of Karachi. However, this study concerns itself only with (1) the land warfare aspect of border defence; (2) the peacetime security of those borders; and (3) the peacetime in-shore security aspect of the coastal defence of Indian's maritime boundaries. The defence of Indian airspace and war-time seaward defence issues are not touched upon. An organisational and operational philosophy is proposed after an examination of the present conditions and the existing general system of defending the border in peace and war.

The suggested solutions for the new realities include suggestions for both border defence and for border security management. In the realm of border defence, a major role for a completely re-organised TA, with a new philosophy and a new operational role is suggested, to augment existing operational planning. The fundamental change would be that the TA would become an active war-fighting force, unlike its present subsidiary role of defending rear-area Vulnerable Areas (VAs) and Vulnerable Points (VPs). In the event of war, the TA, with its predominantly local or regional troops, can be envisaged as fighting against any foreign enemy ingress within their own home region, along with the Regular Army, as the 'first line of defence'. A re-created Army Reserve could additionally be dovetailed into a new system in any of many possible ways. These are examined for their practicality and easy integration into existing defensive policies and operational methods.

This study has two limitations. First, since military operational planning for any defensive tactical battle in various segments of India's borders is understandably not made public, the specifics are not debated herein. Second, while the various sections of the border are described and discussed, the details of the existing security arrangements are as available in open-source publications only. These may not therefore be either wholly accurate or fully up-to-date. Nevertheless, they are grounded in reality, even if the information is not derived from actual ground research undertaken for the purpose of this study, but are from secondary sources. A third factor which needs to be taken into account is that the analysis is that of the author, and is not a compilation of secondary analyses. There could, therefore, be some variation between the author's perceptions and recommendations, and the existing details of deployments and operational plans in some sectors.

## NOTES

1. So termed by the Pakistani Army Chief, Gen Mirza Aslam Beg, on 02 December 1990 at a talk delivered at the annual seminar of the Pakistan Ordnance Factories at Wah Cantonment, near Islamabad. His concept was not explained at the time.
2. 22nd Report of the Parliamentary Standing Committee on Defence (2006-07), 14th Lok Sabha, July 2007, pp. 1-3.
3. 32nd Report of the Parliamentary Standing Committee on Defence (2008-09), December 2008, p. 3.
4. Ibid., pp. 10-4.
5. Partly due to the difficulties with the implementation of the system in the build-up to the 1971 India-Pakistan War, and partly due to the ongoing socio-economic changes in Indian society.
6. Collectively known at present as Personnel Below Officer Rank (PBOR).

# Part I
# BORDERS

CHAPTER 2

# The Sino-Indian Border

## Sino-Indian Border War Threat

India's borders with China, which lie primarily along Tibet's Himalayan interface with the Indian sub-continent, remain *de facto* rather than *de jure*, because there has been no agreement with China on their precise definition. The border has thus not been jointly delimited (i.e. geographically defined) by mutual agreement, and till then, cannot be jointly demarcated. In international *realpolitik*, the dispute regarding the border is only the symptom of a greater dispute, that of territory. China claims almost the entire state of Arunachal Pradesh on the nebulous and dubious basis of her claim of sovereignty over Tibet. This had earlier led to the war of 1962. The territorial dispute is unlikely to get resolved easily, and thus, the border will remain in a state of disagreement for the unforeseeable future, instead of becoming an agreed border. India's relations with China have thawed since 1976, and though there was a period of frostiness after the 1998 Pokhran-II nuclear tests by India, they soon thawed again due to conscious efforts by both countries. The agreement of 1993 for the "maintenance of border peace and tranquility", and that of 1996 on "confidence-building in the military field" are currently operative, and the Sino-Indian frontier is generally peaceful. However, Chinese intrusions continue, perhaps deliberately. Moreover, current Chinese military doctrine and policy include preparing for "high-tech limited war", "active defence", and for a "punitive offensive" with a "minor incursion" into a neighboring country.[1] Indian military preparedness to defend this border, particularly in Arunachal Pradesh and other disputed territories in Himachal Pradesh and Ladakh, therefore, continues to be vital. That the threat from China is being taken seriously again by India is shown by the 2008 decision of the Indian government to raise two more mountain divisions, as reiterated on 15 February 2010 by India's Defence Minister, Mr. AK Antony, while speaking to the press.[2]

The war threat to the Sino-Indian border is thus that of a war initiated by the PRC at a time of its own choosing, to "reclaim" all disputed territory, or to demonstrate its superiority. Such a timing could well be to relieve pressure on Pakistan in the event of an Indo-Pakistan military confrontation or a transition to overt hostilities. A border war could even be initiated by China in order to divert her own population's attention away from domestic economic issues, or as a demonstration or warning for other peripheral countries such as Vietnam. The threat is, therefore, of a conventional ground offensive, supported by missile and air forces and all other elements of modern high-tech war, including cyber-war.[3] The threat has perforce to be met with ground troops tactically deployed to defend all potential routes of ingress, defensive positions in strategic depth areas which fall within China's "claim line", and appropriate planning, as well as all other physical preparations to counter-attack to regain any territory lost. Peace-time deployment of both BGFs and of regular Army troops has necessarily to cater for a quick and easy transition to the planned war deployment posture, which will thus need to cater for the need of prior acclimatisation. To prevent confusion, minimal changes in command and control structure are thus essential. Whether this threat from China is more dangerous or potentially more damaging than the one from Pakistan needs to be assessed carefully, and the necessary military preparations budgeted for accordingly.

An issue that also needs to be factored into the overall planning process for the Sino-Indian border, as also for the Indo-Pakistan border to be discussed later, is that all three countries are nuclear-armed. This is likely to limit the possibility of ground ingress to either a short duration, or alternatively perhaps to a shallow penetration, before the defender's "nuclear threshold" is reached, unless his nuclear capability can be effectively de-graded by some other means. Though both India and China officially have a "No First Use" (NFU) policy, China has qualified it by saying that it does not apply to use within its own territory, which could be applied to its territorial claims in Arunachal Pradesh, for example. At the same time, it has further qualified its NFU policy to say that it only applies to recognised nuclear powers, among which it pointedly does not include India. Therefore, the planning process will need to determine both the geographical and the temporal nuclear thresholds, while deciding upon the necessary deployment pattern.

Meanwhile, India's northern border with China remains free from hostile infiltration during peacetime, thanks to the 1993 and 1996 agreements regarding the border with the PRC. However, China indulges in simultaneously maintaining peace and tranquility on the border with India while keeping up with its military and diplomatic pin-pricks intended to assert its territorial claim to most of the Indian state of Arunachal Pradesh. China thus deliberately follows a carefully-nuanced "blow hot, blow cold" policy towards India, primarily showing its diplomatic "blow cold" smiling face, while retaining the prerogative to "blow hot", either diplomatically or militarily, whenever it suits them. The US and China are now, post-2008, symbiotically linked financially in helping each other weather the economic downturn caused by the recklessness of the US financial market. With its military pre-occupation with Afghanistan forcing it to maintain Pakistan as a most-favoured non-NATO military ally, any future American diplomatic assistance in addressing India's security concerns *vis-à-vis* both Pakistan and China is likely to be illusory. India, therefore, has to be both self-reliant and realistic, in examining its defensive options.

## Defensive Options

### *J&K*

The Sino-Indian border in J&K is with two of the PRC's regions, the Xinjiang-Uighur Autonomous Region (Xinjiang, for short), also known earlier as Chinese Turkestan or Eastern Turkestan, and the Tibet Autonomous Region (TAR). J&K's northern border is with Xinjiang,[4] the agreed boundary passing through the Karakoram Pass, while the eastern border, presently disputed and thus not yet agreed upon, is with the TAR. A large expanse of inhospitable territory known as Aksai Chin,[5] falls within what India believes is part of the erstwhile state of J&K. However, because of its importance to the PRC in providing a surface link between the two regions, it has been occupied by it since the mid-1950s. The Chinese "claim lines" include this territory within the PRC, and in the 1962 war, the Chinese PLA actually drove the scanty Indian forces backs westwards of their claimed boundary. This general line now is an ill-defined LAC, on either side of which the two sides now patrol or occupy permanent military positions. In spite of ongoing border negotiations through meetings of a Joint Working Group (JWG), the PRC has not clarified what in their opinion is the precise alignment of the LAC. Neither border is presently subject to constant military threat, or even to a creeping forward or "nibbling" capture of additional territory by either side. PLA strengths and dispositions across the border in both the Xinjiang Military Region and the Tibet Military District (TMD) are indicative of the PLA's ability to fight for the possession of their claimed boundaries. In addition, the massive build-up of infrastructure all over the Tibetan plateau indicates an ability to both induct much larger numbers of troops into the TAR, and to conduct offensive operations into Indian territory, in keeping with its current "Active Defence" philosophy. China's infrastructure developments in Western Tibet (Ngari Prefecture) in particular are well beyond its possible defensive needs. Taken in conjunction with the presence of Chinese personnel in Northern POK,[6] and the ongoing up-gradation of the Karakoram Highway linking Xinjiang to Pakistan, these simultaneous developments are undoubtedly worrisome. Indian defensive dispositions are based on its defensive philosophy, with the aim of preventing any further westward advance of Chinese forces into Ladakh. Any alternative military option would have to be based on a change in India's diplomatic strategy *vis-a-vis* the PRC. This is a vast subject by itself and cannot be discussed here, but any eventual agreement on these boundaries, would possibly allow a reduction in troops required for defensive purposes. Within the existing diplomatic and military posture adopted by India, there exist some modifying options: (1) a greater reliance on technological advances in surveillance to cover the open expanses of the disputed Tibet frontier; (2) more dedicated air effort for both surveillance and ground attack, including the building of additional military airfields in Ladakh.[7] These should permit forward basing of both helicopters and appropriate fixed-wing fighter aircraft. A light-weight, all-weather, modern multi-role combat aircraft, which is designed and constructed for extreme cold weather basing with minimal maintenance support at austere locations, would be particularly suitable. Such an aircraft available off-the-shelf at present is the Swedish Saab JAS 39 Gripen NG,[8] a "4.5$^{th}$-generation fighter". Dedicated ground-attack Close Air Support (CAS) aircraft like the US A-10 "Warthog" and attack helicopters in addition would be desirable. As a simultaneous diplomatic nuance, India will require to display more self-confidence and resoluteness than it does at present.

*Himachal Pradesh and Uttarakhand*

There is less of a territorial dispute along the Sino-Indian frontier in these two states, though there are a few disputed areas. Much of the boundary is in fact agreed upon. Consequently, the diplomatic stakes for both countries are much lower. The existing military contingency planning should be appropriate. The situation does not require discussion of any major alternative options.

*Sikkim*

The PRC has not yet formally accepted the integration of Sikkim into the Indian Union,[9] which occurred in 1975 through a popular democratic majority decision of its inhabitants. After the Sikkim-British India Treaty of Titaliya of February 1817, Sikkim had formally become a British Protectorate in 1861, which was recognised by China in 1890. From then till 1947, Sikkim had been a protectorate of British India, though this was disputed by Tibet,[10] and from 1947 to 1975, Sikkim had been an Indian protectorate. The PRC, since its creation in 1949, has not accepted the Indian possession of Sikkim, on the basis of its (China's) claim to sovereignty over Tibet. It has, however, not yet tried to take Sikkim by force. Part of the reason for this is that the present Sikkim-Tibet boundary was agreed upon between Britain and Imperial China on 17 March 1890. Till the 1962 Sino-Indian war, there were no significant planned Indian military defensive deployments. The present planning and preparations envisage the defence of the boundary. Since the PRC deliberately disputes minor points along even this agreed boundary, along which armed clashes have taken place in 1967, a future use of force by the PRC cannot be ruled out. As such, alternative military options do not appear to exist.

*Arunachal Pradesh*

The disputed Sino-Indian boundary in Arunachal Pradesh is in reality not a "border dispute" *per se*, but actually an intractable territorial dispute over ownership of most of Arunachal Pradesh. The "border" part of the dispute relates to the dispute over the alignment of the McMahon Line, a tentative British Indian 1913 delineation of the Indo-Tibet boundary. Signed between Tibet and British India in 1914, it was never recognised by the Chinese Government. China had not recognised it at the time of its inception, believing that it still had suzerainty over Tibet, which had conditionally accepted it. This line was based on the geographical principle of a line generally following the highest crest-lines[11] of the Himalayas along the southern edge of the Tibetan plateau.[12] The "border" along the McMahon Line is 1,030 kms-long, and nevertheless continues as the *de facto* border, in spite of the PRC's calling it "the illegal McMahon Line". The entire issue was part of the background that led to the 1962 war. It is still the most vexatious issue between India and China. Given that India and China have already been to war once over this issue, and China remains both obdurate and occasionally belligerent on the issue, military defensive preparations for the defence of the *de facto* boundary or LAC remain imperative. The most-threatened area is the Kameng sector, which includes the Tawang District with the prestigious monastery.

As far as the war in October 1962 in this sector is concerned, the Indian Army's faulty dispositions caused a serious military reverse, mainly due to the forward defending brigade being deployed a hundred kilometres away to the west of Tawang, along the Namka Chu rivulet. The November 1962 debacle at Sela, further south towards the Assam plains, was caused by poor generalship. Even today, there is perhaps no major alternative military option but to continue with defensive planning and preparations to defend both Tawang itself, and the entire Tawang-Sela-Bomdila axis. Only a complete agreement with the PRC on the entire Indo-Tibet border will allow India to lower its guard. However, alternate military options within the totality of full preparedness do appear to be feasible. Such options, or sub-options, within the present military posture, will revolve around how far forward the local holding division's main defences should be.[13] This is a debate that has existed since the defence of the Kameng sector was first contemplated in early 1962, and created both controversy and chaos during the October-November 1962 Chinese attack. Sela is undoubtedly the best defensive position along the axis Tawang-Sela-Bomdila, and needs to be held in strength. Nevertheless, the question of the defence of Tawang monastery and town is politically and diplomatically important. The Tawang township is barely 30 kilometres aerial distance from the *de facto* Indo-Tibetan border at Bumla, on the edge of the Tibetan plateau. Therefore, the tactical requirement of securing the monastery and town will require adequate defensive strength located forward. This needs to be catered for even under the present Border Management Policy and an assessed "low-level threat" scenario. There is also one administrative issue related to the tactical and operational defence planning for this sector, which merits attention. This is the question of the deployments of BGFs in peace-time, which are to come under the Army's operational command and control on the outbreak of hostilities. Given their role, arms and equipment, organisational ethos and type of training, these BGFs cannot be expected to fulfill a covering troops' role. Such a role envisages them fighting delaying operations in what for them will be a withdrawal operation of war, one of the most difficult operations to carry out. In the extremely difficult and steep Himalayan terrain and its extreme climate at most times of the year, such an expectation would be militarily unrealistic.

## Peace-time Requirements

The military problems associated with the defence of this sensitive 3,488 kms-long *de facto* border[14] have been examined above. The peace-time security problems are relatively low, but the arrangements made for them are not fully satisfactory as yet, as has been brought out earlier. The ITBP is the nominated BGF for the security of this long frontier, as per the "One Border, One Force" policy, but that has been difficult to practice in totality, because this border also simultaneously remains a responsibility of the AR. The ITBP is deployed from Diphu La in Arunachal Pradesh to the Karakoram Pass area in J&K. The political nature of the territorial problem with China renders this border sensitive to any sudden action by China. This automatically necessitates a large Army presence in the forward border zone, with peace-time defensive deployments both right along the disputed McMahon Line and also in depth behind these forward deployments as a Rapid Reaction Force. The ITBP has six battalions deployed in Arunachal Pradesh.[15] In the eastern sector of the border, there is also some deployment of the traditional BGF for the frontier, the AR, which has BOPs under the Army's operational control. Thus, there is a mixed deployment of ITBP, a BGF under the MHA, infantry units of the Army, and of AR, a force belonging to the MHA but officered by Army officers and placed under Army operational control—a complex mix which does not, generally speaking, augur well for speedy redeployments and changes in command and control structure during a sudden transition to a war-fighting posture. If such a transition is to be carried out under active enemy interference, whether physical, electronic, or cyber-war, the result would likely be chaos. If this is to be carried out in the face of a sudden and unexpected Chinese attack, it is a sure-fire recipe for disaster.

## Notes

1. Gurmeet Kanwal, *Indian Army Vision 2020* (New Delhi: Harper Collins, 2008), pp. 149-50.
2. "Indian Army raising two divisions close to China border," *DNA*, 15 February 2010, http://www.dnaindia.com/india/report_indian-army-raising-two-divisions-close-to-china-border_1348336, accessed on 16 February 2010.
3. China's unparalleled asymmetric warfare capability in the field of cyber warfare has, in some senses, reduced the earlier importance of the physical geographic borders. A trans-border war can thus be launched without the physical ingress of ground troops, a factor worth noting in the diplomatic-legal sphere.
4. Spelt "Sinkiang" in older literature.
5. A Turkic name and not a Tibetan name; the disputed area lies between the two cultural regions.
6. See Selig S. Harrison, "China's Discreet Hold on Pakistan's Northern Borderlands," *New York Times*, 26 August 2010.
7. This has in fact belatedly been under way from 2008 onwards, with Advanced Landing Grounds (ALGs) being made operational at Daulat Beg Oldi (DBO), Fukche, and Nyoma, as reported in the Indian media in 2009. See, for example, "Air Force steps up LAC defence," *Hindustan Times*, 26 September 2009.
8. Though a single-engined aircraft, which on the plus side, makes it easier to maintain than twin-engine aircraft, it is the only "4th+ generation" fighter aircraft in the MMRCA competition for the IAF, and the only one specifically designed for cold-climate maintenance at less-developed airbases such as Leh.
9. Though, as of 2010, some of the maps emanating from the PRC are no longer showing Sikkim as Chinese territory under the illegal occupation of India.
10. Imperial China had exercised suzerainty over Tibet till 1911, when the Manchu empire collapsed, following which Tibet formally declared its independence from China in 1913.
11. Often wrongly described as following the "Watershed Principle".
12. For details of this discussion and the Tibet-British India Shimla Agreement of 1914, see Gautam Das, *China-Tibet-India: The 1962 War and the Strategic Military Future* (New Delhi: Har-Anand Publications, 2009), pp. 67-76 and pp. 127-9.
13. "Exercise LAL QILA" had first been carried out in 1960 by the then GOC-in-C Eastern Command, Lt Gen SPP Thorat to consider the Chinese threat. He had earlier been the corps commander responsible for the sector, prior to the forward deployment, and was well aware of the ground realities.
14. As per "Origin of ITBP—The "Himveers" and National Security," *Indo-Tibetan Border Police Force*, http://itbpolice.nic.in/mar.htm, accessed on 21 July 2009.
15. Ibid.

CHAPTER 3

# The Indo-Pakistan Borders

A significant part of the problem relating to the defence of the Indo-Pakistan borders, comprising both the accepted IB and the alignment in the disputed state of J&K, stems from the attitude of the Pakistan Army towards the Indian state. While it justifies its hostility to India to its own public by maintaining that India is a constant military threat to the existence of Pakistan, it uses this to bolster its own hold on the governance of Pakistan and retain control of Pakistan's foreign and defence policy. To appreciate the varied nature of the threat to the Indo-Pakistani border, it will be useful to understand Pakistan's military policy towards India. This was first articulated by Gen Mirza Aslam Beg, who was Pakistan's Army Chief from 1988 to mid-1991.

## Pakistan's "Strategic Defiance" against India

"Strategic Defiance" is a term coined by Gen Mirza Aslam Beg,[1] an emotive phrase to describe Pakistan's "peace-time" activities against India, which can be said to be that country's present standard operating policy. The entire spectrum of hostile activities in what may be termed "cold peace" conditions constitutes the peace-time range of actions directed against India. It includes use of its so-called "strategic assets": the various fundamentalist Islamic terrorist *jihadi* groups. These armed *lashkars* can be used in "cold peace" as instruments of proxy war, as well as in "hot war" situations, both in conjunction with Pakistani military operational planning and also on their own, across less-defended sectors of the Indo-Pakistan border. Inciting stone-pelting street mobs in the Kashmir Valley through the use of infiltrated and local instigators is also part of the range of the peace-time activities, though not directly related to border defence. This peace-time policy, and the array of inimical actions it connotes, is part of a larger whole: an entire spectrum of hostile armed actions against India that would continue from peace-time into war, orchestrated and conducted by the Pakistan armed forces. This may be called Pakistan's "New-Generation Warfare" (NGW).

## Pakistan's "New-Generation Warfare"

Central to an understanding of the challenge faced by the Indian national security planners and by the armed forces of India is the scope and nature of Pakistan's functional anti-India military philosophy for both peace and war conditions. The term NGW is being used to describe a simultaneous combination of offensive actions that is being used by the Pakistani state since the Pokhran-II and Chagai nuclear tests of 1998 in its ongoing, though unofficial, war against India. NGW also encompasses a method of combining all these actions with conventional military operations, special forces' operations, and the threat or actual use of both strategic and battlefield (or "tactical") nuclear weapons. NGW, therefore, is a functioning methodology or the flexible combination of a number of offensive methods, which is being used for over a decade by Pakistan in putting into action its hostility against India. NGW can thus be said to be a spectrum of offensive actions employing a variable but simultaneous combination of:

- Nuclear blackmail at the strategic level; Pakistan's so-called "low nuclear threshold"—This is primarily directed against "high-value" targets, i.e. cities, by threatening the use of "city-buster" nuclear weapons. The delivery means available to Pakistan for such a threatened use include both missiles and aircraft.
- A low-intensity Pakistani-sponsored insurgency or "proxy war" in the state of J&K, conducted by a combination of Kashmiri Islamic militants, and foreign *jihadis*, mainly Pakistanis—This is what Pakistan calls the "Kashmiri freedom movement", and which is being contested by the Indian security forces in Low Intensity Conflict Operations (LICO) against "Anti-National Elements" (ANE's).
- Pakistan-condoned cross-border terrorism by supposedly "non-state actors" within the interior of India, as in the attack on the Indian Parliament on 13 December 2001, and the Mumbai episode of 26 November 2008—Such groups could also undertake raids on Indian wartime rear area military facilities and ambushes of military supply and replenishment railway traffic and road convoys.

- Internally-generated but Pakistan-supported terrorism, as in the Mumbai serial train blasts of 11 July 2006.
- Cross-LoC armed intrusions in J&K for capture of additional territory, as exemplified by the incursion of 1999 in the Kargil area. These are what Pakistan's former Army Chief and President, Gen Pervez Musharraf, has described as "Aggressive Patrolling".
- Special Forces operations against a variety of strategic and combat zone military targets, combining air, sea and land methods of insertion and extraction.
- Conventional tactical military and naval operations, in conjunction with integrated air operations, as well as independent air operations—These would employ tactical or operational Surface-to-Surface Missiles (SSM) with conventional warheads against military targets, whether battlefield targets or base area facilities.
- Use of low-yield Tactical Nuclear Weapons (TNW) against battlefield targets—It would also include the detonation of TNW in the atmosphere in order to produce an Electro-Magnetic Pulse (EMP), which would make all modern digital and other communication equipment inoperable.

Thus we see that in the future, any "border war" with Pakistan would most likely also be a war in the interiors of India, and against all of a wide variety of "soft" targets which are normally left unprotected because they have not been targeted in the past. Any future armed conflict with Pakistan will most likely be fought over the entire spectrum of modern warfare from cyber-war to the threat or actual use of nuclear weapons, and spatially both deep within the country as well as close to the borders. The region has entered a new age of "no-holds barred" warfare at a sub-nuclear level, which will simultaneously completely occupy the police, the para-military forces and the armed forces. Clearly, therefore, any border defence policy for the Indo-Pakistan border needs to take the entire spectrum of threat into account, even while specifically catering for a physical defence of the geographical boundaries of India.

## Cross-border Attacks by Non-state Actors and "Swarming" Tactics

Because non-state actors have not played any role outside J&K in the past wars with Pakistan, the possible nature of their likely attacks needs to be considered. After the Pakistan-based *jihadi* attack on Mumbai on 26 November 2008, Pakistan itself has been rapidly sliding into instability, as the fundamentalist Islamic forces have been gaining ground. These elements have openly declared their hostility to and their intention of attacking India. Though the Pakistan Army has, apparently reluctantly, undertaken operations against the mainly-Pathan Pakistani Taliban in parts of the province of Khyber Pakhtunkhwa,[2] its own linkages to fundamental *jihadi* elements will remain, and can be used by them to divert their attention to Indian targets, both in disputed Kashmir and elsewhere. Such *jihadi* elements have long declared that their enemies are America, Israel and India, and the dispatch of armed groups into India is but the next step. Simultaneously, the rise of the non-Pathan Taliban in the form of the Tehrik-e-Taliban Pakistan (TTP) and its increasing influence in the Punjab province, particularly in the poorer southern Punjab,[3] has also become a serious cause of concern for India because of its rabidly anti-Indian orientation.

The operations of the Pakistan Army that began in May 2009, after the breakdown of the Swat Accord with other fundamentalist elements, resulted in the rallying of all such like-minded fundamentalist Islamic organisations from the Federally Administered Tribal Areas (FATA), the Provincially Administered Tribal Areas (PATA), and the rest of the NWFP and the Punjab, coalescing to fight the army. If Pakistan were to create a war-threat from India, all the *jihadi* elements could join hands at any time for anti-India operations. That this is no idle conjecture is evident from the fact that Mullah Omar had promised Pakistan 50,000 Taliban fighters to fight against India if Pakistan wanted.

All activities against India may or may not be directly sponsored by the Pakistani Government, but all indications are that they are being encouraged and supported. The Lashkar-e-Tayyeba (LeT) and Jaish-e-Mohammed (JeM) are often in the news because their leaders make blatant public statements regarding their intentions to attack India. In fact, the strategic stalemate resulting from Pakistan's possession of nuclear weapons, which has greatly offset India's conventional superiority, makes the possibility of attacks by non-state actors more likely than conventional military action. This phenomenon has been described as the "Stability-Instability Paradox".[4] All this is nothing new, but what needs to be examined is the likely method of their attacking targets in India.

Commando-style raids, as demonstrated in Mumbai in November 2008, require detailed planning and lengthy preparation and training. A few more such can be expected in any warlike situation between India and Pakistan. Some such could even be executed, with ISI guidance in planning, against Indian military HQ in rear areas and their communication facilities. However, the most likely cross-border *jihadi* attacks are those that require the least preparation and lead time. These are likely to be cross-border penetrations in the thinly-held segments of the Indo-Pakistan IB, and possibly even mounted across the Indo-Nepal border. The tactical methods could vary from military-style attacks on lightly-held border outposts of the BGFs, to terrorist-type attacks in the immediate rear of the border, on civilian targets and Indian government communications facilities, to attacks on military administrative rear establishments. The choice of suitable and lucrative targets is vast and varied. The simplest tactical method for use by non-military armed groups with ample manpower is that of "swarming", broadly, the overwhelming of an objective by simultaneous attacks on various parts of it, all mounted from different directions. The applicability of this method extends to simultaneous attacks on a number of different smaller objectives within a specific area, leading to confusion among the defenders at all levels.[5] The only antidote to such attacks is to have the defensive arrangements under one cohesive system, and to have large numbers of available reserve forces at every level—both requirements may necessitate changes to the existing systems. Wartime control of all defensive forces and reserve or "second line" forces need to be vested in the MoD, and commanded at the local levels by the relevant sector commanders of the Army, under the Army's local area, zonal and theatre formation HQ, going upwards in a single chain of command. A manifold increase in the Reserve and "second line" forces is also urgently necessary, including an increase in the TA in all border and coastal states, as well as the re-creation of an Army Reserve. Both the command system and the increased reserves need to be dovetailed into a new contingency defensive planning, which needs to incorporate the BGFs, the Army, and the local civil government. To do this requires an understanding of the development of the present existing system.

## Evolution of the Defensive System along the Indo-Pakistan International Border

Till 1965, India's borders with Pakistan were manned by the respective State Armed Police and the CRPF. On 9 April 1965, Pakistan attacked Sardar Post, Chhar Bet and Beria Bet in the Rann of Kutch region, and captured the Sardar Border Outpost manned by the Gujarat Armed Police. Indian Army troops from the brigade at Jamnagar were then hastily inducted into the sector. Pakistan's launched its "Operation DESERT HAWK" using its 18 Infantry Division under Maj Gen Tikka Khan, with two armoured regiments[6] newly-equipped with American-supplied M-47 and M-48 Patton tanks. The Pakistani offensive pushed back the Indian forces and penetrated well into Indian territory, right up to Biar Bet. The Army Chief Gen JN Chaudhuri decided that, other than for a holding operation, the ground and overall situation in the Rann of Kutch area was not suitable for a proper defensive battle, and advised the Prime Minister Lal Bahadur Shastri accordingly. Shastri decided to allow the Army the freedom to decide its own response. The Indian Army reacted by mobilising its field formations in the Punjab as a counterpoise in order to relieve the pressure on Kutch.[7]

The Pakistan Army had been pleased with its performance in Kutch[8] and was thus encouraged to press on with its plans for the attack by infiltration into J&K later that year, code-named "Operation GIBRALTAR". On the Indian side, in May 1965, Lt Gen Harbaksh Singh, GOC-in-C Western Command, had deployed defensively facing the international border, as per the military teachings of the time. These were British concepts from the Second World War, used by their armies in battles around the world.[9] The main defences were brigade defended sectors in depth along the likely Pakistani routes of ingress, up to 30-35 kms within own territory, and based mostly on communications centres. The defensive layout provided for only a thin screen of troops ahead, and due to the distances between these defended sectors, it forced a mathematical distribution of anti-tank mines, armour and supporting arms. The defences were not based on obstacles such as the canals and drainages that existed in the area. There was thus a high possibility of Pakistani armour penetrating deep into Indian territory and of some defended sectors being either by-passed or over-run. Reviewing this deployment, Gen JN Chaudhuri changed the deployment pattern to a more forward posture so as to not lose any territory. The new deployments were based on the existing obstacles for optimum utilisation of their anti-tank potential. Armour was to be concentrated in suitable locations to meet enemy thrusts from the flanks and rear. The new philosophy was to take the war into Pakistani territory as far as possible, to provide a cushion for sensitive Indian territory.[10] In essence therefore, the Indian territorial defence policy along the Pakistan border in the Punjab and northern Rajasthan has remained the same from the second half of 1965 onwards.

Distributing the available force along a linear front based on one or more canal or other linear obstacles inevitably brings up an associated problem: If all or most of the force is up ahead, there will be a near-vacuum behind the thin crust of the defence, and nothing substantial to block any significant enemy thrust which manages to penetrate. This is an age-old military dilemma from before the age of firearms. A fresh thought was given to this problem by Lt Gen PS Bhagat, VC, when he was a Corps Commander in the Punjab. His solution was to become the defensive concept for the Punjab for the decades to follow, proving effective even in the 1971 war[11] that ensued soon after its inception.

Gen Bhagat got the views of commanders, down to the unit level, regarding the tactical difficulties they faced in their defensive operational role. He also asked politicians for their opinions regarding the possible initial loss of territory, and met a cross-section of the local population to assess their reactions on the same subject. Neither the politicians nor the local population were prepared to risk the overrunning of their territory by Pakistan even briefly. He assessed that Pakistan could take the initiative to start a war. It was therefore necessary to defend the border as far forward as possible to ensure that Pakistan did not gain territory in the initial rush before the Indian forces went into action.

Maj Gen Sukhwant Singh writes:

> Bhagat also realised that occasions might arise where it might be difficult to regain lost territory within the tight schedule of a short war, and this would prove embarrassing in post-war bargaining. He therefore argued that an extensive system should be created all along the border to prevent Pakistan from rushing the border defences to develop deeper thrusts towards the interior of India. For this purpose, he created a defensive system in Punjab, which later came to be known as the "ditch-cum-bund" (DCB) type of defence.[12]

The DCB system of defences has come to stay in the areas wherever it has been built, and its presence both influences and dictates the military policy of border defence as well as its operational methodology. Since it continues to be germane to the existing situation and to this study, an understanding of the tactical theory underlying the DCB defence system is required. It consists of an anti-tank ditch of a width which could not be negotiated by a bridge-laying tank and would need a deliberate bridging effort to cross. The ditch is covered (*by fire*)[13] by a high bund, housing concrete fortifications, from where coordinated anti-tank fire as well as machine-gun and small-arms fire can be brought to bear on enemy troops approaching and negotiating the ditch.

The aim of the DCB system as developed was to force an attacking force to establish a proper tactical bridgehead to eliminate small-arms fire, and then to construct a bridge to enable armour to be built up across the ditch, from where it could stage a breakout into the rear areas. The concept of defensive operations visualised that by successive interference and delay caused in negotiating the ditch, the invader would not be able to build up any sizable force of armour across the obstacle in daytime. From the time-frame required to achieve this, it was presupposed that the construction of a bridge would invariably be carried out in darkness, especially in conditions of air parity. Gen Bhagat propounded that the attacker would be eliminated piecemeal in the process of building up across the ditch, where his full potential could not be brought into play.[14]

Bhagat's arguments convinced the Army Chief Gen PP Kumaramangalam, and the national political leadership, and thus a major part of the Punjab border was so fortified before the next war with Pakistan in 1971. Many have disagreed with this system of defensive planning, calling it the result of a "Maginot Line mentality"; a thin crust which could be breached with disastrous results. However, the tendency towards the "Fortress India" type of defensive layout has continued, being further strengthened and extended by the fencing of the entire Indo-Pakistan IB and the greater portion of the LoC. Any and every system has its own advantages and drawbacks; the efficacy of this combination lies in the reduction of cross-border infiltration in peace-time, and the best manner of defending the western border in a "Great Wall of India" tactical fashion. In the present circumstances of an India-Pakistan strategic "Stability-Instability Paradox", its major shortcoming appears to lie in its inescapable requirement of much larger numbers of trained and rehearsed military manpower available nearby at very short notice.

## The War Threat

The Indo-Pakistan border is divided into two different types: an International Border (IB) which both recognise and is demarcated on ground, and a politically and militarily disputed border within the erstwhile princely state of J&K. While the IB is located in the plains and constitutes the western edge of the Indian states of Gujarat, Rajasthan, Punjab and a small part of J&K, the disputed borders in J&K lie in mountainous terrain. This disputed frontline is divided between what are called a LoC and an AGPL in the area of the Siachen Glacier. The LoC-AGPL is an "active" border with a constant threat of armed incursions from across it, both by armed terrorists who are supposedly "non-state actors" supported covertly by the Pakistan Government, or directly by the Pakistan Army itself. The last major incursion resulted in the Kargil "war" or border battles of May to July 1999, in which both the Indian Army and the Air Force had to be used to evict the intruders. The problem for India in J&K is exacerbated by the existence of a separatist insurgency within the Kashmir Valley and some adjacent areas, which is fomented and supported by Pakistan as a "proxy war" of low-intensity conflict (LIC). This complicates the practical issue of the deployment of military and para-military forces in the LIC-affected areas lying adjacent to the LoC. The Army's own specialist COIN force, the Rashtriya Rifles (RR), is deployed in the interiors of J&K, along with some other elements of the Army, to deal with the COIN requirement. The Army's regular infantry battalions are deployed along the LoC, with a few BSF companies augmenting this deployment in a few locations. The IB itself, however, is protected in peace-time by the BSF. The limited Army presence is located in some forward cantonments, while the bulk of dedicated Army defensive resources are located further back.

The two different major segments of the Indo-Pakistan border in J&K face two different types of war threat due to both their politico-legal differences and their terrain difference. In the plains sector, in the present circumstances, the IB is under threat of a conventional military offensive only if the political situation between the two countries spins totally out of control. Such an offensive would most probably be armour-heavy, and supported by offensive air support both in terms of CAS as well as counter-air operations against Indian air bases. The aim of such an offensive would most likely be to capture maximum Indian territory for post-war bargaining, rather than yet another attempt to capture Akhnur and cut the Jammu-Poonch road, as was the aim both in 1965 and in 1971. Given a situation of nuclear near-parity, such an offensive might be shallow but could be fairly extensive, rather than an attempted deep penetration. The defensive border war scenario described in the previous chapter would be the likely pattern of Indian operations, where speed in defensive reaction would be of essence. Other than that, the military problem is one of presenting the strongest possible forward defensive posture, while simultaneously maintaining ample reserves for both counter-penetration and for local counter-attacks, held sufficiently far forward to react in the shortest possible time.

The war threat to the LoC-AGPL could take the form of a conventional mountain warfare offensive, combining regular infantry and special forces operations in depth, or commando raids, supported by whatever air support the terrain and available platforms permit. It could also be combined with complimentary or supplementary attacks in the interior by "non-state actors" and their local collaborators of the fundamentalist Islamic/separatist variety. The military problem is one which requires an availability of adequate troops holding ground in all tactically important areas along or close behind the LoC-AGPL, as also having available an adequate reserve kept ready nearby for the quickest-possible counter-attack. Such counter-attacks could be either defensive, to regain lost features and territory, or offensive, to carry the war into enemy-held territory. As in the case of the Sino-Indian border region, peace-time deployments of both BGFs and forward-located/deployed regular troops should be made in a way that facilitates fast and easy transition to the planned war deployment. Equally, to prevent confusion and facilitate speed of reaction, minimal changes in command and control structures is essential in the transition from peace to war scenarios, again as in the Sino-Indian border areas.

## Defensive Options

### *The Indo-Pakistan IB*

This runs from the Sir Creek area in the Rann of Kutch in Gujarat, northwards through Rajasthan and Punjab, and into the state of J&K, till it meets the LoC where it begins. A militarily passive border, it is watched over in peace-time by the BSF, which has 609 BOPs located along it.[15] On the Pakistan side, a similar BGF, the Pakistan Rangers, performs the same functions. War-time deployment of the Army has, over the years, crystallised into a policy of holding a 'thin crust' type of defence based on obstacles, as earlier described. Reserves are concentrated for counter-attacks and larger forces are mobilised and held concentrated for an offensive counter-strike, which requires political will and appropriate corresponding diplomatic effort. The only different alternate option has been discarded due to the political necessity of "no loss of territory is acceptable". This alternative requires the concentration and employment of greater offensive forces, created by not deploying a large proportion of the available forces on the forward linear defences. If such a choice is not to be exercised, then ways and means need to be found to quickly further thicken the forward "thin crust" deployment, through augmentation by newly-created defensive military forces. A total re-orientation and re-organisation of the TA is a feasible method to do this.

### *The LoC and AGPL in J&K*

The Simla Agreement of 02 July 1972 was arrived at after the 1971 Indo-Pakistan war, in which India emerged decisively victorious. It stipulated and created an agreed and jointly-demarcated LoC that was not to be violated. This agreement was broken by Pakistan by the Kargil intrusions in 1999, which have in effect put an end to the agreement. This has thus gone the way of the 27 July 1949 Karachi Cease-Fire agreement, which sanctified the earlier CFL.[16] The 1949 agreement was violated by Pakistan in early August 1965 when it launched its "Operation GIBRALTAR", an attack by infiltration across the CFL. Both these agreements are now dead letters, of no diplomatic validity. The present military position along the LoC-AGPL is that of two men pushing at each other with maximum possible strength, one to acquire more of the disputed territory, and the other to prevent it, and remaining static as a result. Neither can afford to ease the pressure, for fear of being pushed back. By continuing to affirm adherence to the Simla Agreement, India has allowed the military advantage to shift to Pakistan, which can afford to deploy lesser forces to physically safeguard the LoC. As an alternative, should India adopt an avowedly aggressive foreign policy regarding J&K, it is Pakistan which will militarily be put on the defensive. This available option requires a concomitant retaliatory policy for LoC transgressions. As an alternate option for India, this has numerous and significant advantages, not least of which is that the military and diplomatic initiative is always retained by India. It will require a corresponding change in logistical support capabilities. A second available option is a diplomatic option that (1) Negotiates agreement on withdrawals by both sides from the AGPL, in the Siachen glacier zone, leading to its de-militarisation; and/or (2) Reaches an agreement on de-militarisation of the entire LoC-AGPL, as once suggested by erstwhile Pakistani President Gen Pervez Musharraf, as one of his many seemingly off-the-cuff proposals. However, in the absence of mutual trust and confidence on both sides, probably well-founded, this entire second option is likely to be a non-starter. As matters stand, the Indian forces available for defence include the large complement of the Army's COIN-oriented RR battalions, which form a viable "second line of defence" and can quickly and easily convert to a defensive posture, utilising their available manpower to advantage

## Peace-time Requirements

Under normal peace-time conditions, the entire Indo-Pakistan IB is secured by the designated BGF, the BSF, which has 609 BOPs located along it, and there are 126 more sanctioned in order to reduce the inter-BOP distance.[17]

### *The LoC and Indo-Pakistan Border in J&K*

The peace-time security requirement for this most-militarised border is no different from its war-time requirement. The permanent extensive defensive deployment has made it a fortified border, with fencing and electronic, aerial and human surveillance at all times, in the effort to prevent crossing of militants. In effect, the J&K border zone is in a permanent war-time operational situation. The Pakistan-abetted and supported LIC in J&K is as much a peace-time problem as it could be in time of war. Among the CPF which are being employed in the State, in addition to the CRPF which is deployed in the interior in IS Duties for the urban areas, there is the BSF. This has now reverted purely to its BGF role. In many sectors of this border, excluding along the AGPL in the Siachen Glacier area, there are BSF battalions or detached companies holding less-threatened sub-sectors under Army control. In spite of the war-like situation, the administration and logistics of the two organisations are entirely different, an unnecessary duplication in the national effort to control militancy. It has been so ever since the BSF was first inducted into the State, soon after its creation in 1965. This is essentially because the two organisations come under two different parent Central ministries, the Army being part of the MoD, while the BSF comes under the MHA. Each has different accounting systems which do not allow the logistical effort to be centralised. A system of command and control within the border zone has been worked out. Unfortunately, the working relationship between the BSF and the Army, which grew increasingly strained since the founding years, has actually become more strained after the GoM designated the BSF as the nodal force to manage the IB opposite Pakistan and Bangladesh. Obviously, the mistakes are on both sides. The main lacuna is however flawed channels of reporting and therefore about accountability. (J&K also has the deployment of another Central BGF, the ITBP, along its north-eastern flank, which was discussed earlier). In J&K, there is certainly ample scope for rationalising some of the Army-CPMF relationship, particularly for the BSF deployed under Army control along the LoC.

There is a portion of the IB in J&K, in the Jammu sector, which has not become part of the LoC. This runs northwards from the Punjab border for 198 kms, till it meets the LoC. In this sector, the BSF is not under the operational control of the Army in peace-time, and is singly responsible for the peace-time security of the IB. Its border-guarding task remains the same as along the LoC, i.e. primarily to prevent infiltration of militants, which is often attempted by Pakistan under the cover of firing from the Pakistani side. Though the IB has been fenced, the terrain is rough, with many rivers and water-courses crossing it, making infiltration easy. Till 2002, the BSF deployment gave each battalion about 30 kms of border, but given the rough terrain and the short approach to the national highway and the railway line, it is a sensitive and vulnerable sector. Four more battalions would have allowed the BSF the latitude to deploy an adequate number of ambushes every night.[18] It is likely that the BSF has now got a more favourable troops-to-task situation. The existing command and control arrangements are on the same lines as for the IB in the Punjab, Rajasthan and Gujarat, for which the BSF is also responsible in peace-time.

### *The Indo-Pakistan Border in Punjab, Rajasthan and Gujarat*

The BSF is the BGF responsible for this approximately 2,177 kms-long border, which has been fenced for most of its length. Arrangements have been made for lighting of the border fence, which has increased the efficacy of the fence as a barrier and deterrent to crossing. The terrain goes from agricultural country cultivated right up to the border, to partly-cultivated semi-desert, sandy desert, and finally to the Rann of Kutch and the creeks running down to the Arabian Sea. The border is 555 kms-long in Punjab, about 1,100 kms in Rajasthan, and 552 kms in Gujarat. The sandy desert is in the Bikaner

Sector (332 kms), the Jaisalmer Sector (525 kms), the Barmer Sector (243 kms of Rajasthan), and the Banaskantha District of Gujarat (190 kms). The peace-time responsibility is to prevent infiltration of militants, prevention of smuggling (mainly of narcotics), and the other routine border security tasks. Along this entire stretch of the IB, the BSF does not normally come under the operational control of the Army anywhere in peace-time. Only exceptionally are some less-threatened BOPs left manned when the Army takes over the border in specific areas in war. The arrangements are generally sound, and the transition to war-time status is unlikely to be problematic. The only very different areas terrain-wise are unfenced portions in the Rann of Kutch and the "Creek area" with salt-water creeks running inland from the sea. The IB in the Kutch District is 332 kms-long. It includes the final 104 kms, where the boundary is disputed by Pakistan, the last 64 kms of which runs along the Sir Creek to the Arabian Sea. The physically difficult creek area is policed by the Water Wing of the BSF along with six BSF battalions, and includes innovative measures such as deploying floating BOPs.[19]

## NOTES

1. See Brian Cloughley, *A History of the Pakistan Army; Wars and Insurrections* (Karachi: Oxford University Press, 2002), pp. 309-13.
2. The recently re-named former NWFP.
3. Lt Gen Nasir Akhtar (Retd), Pakistan Army, former Pakistan 5 Corps Commander in Sind; during a meeting with this author at Lahore on 15 December 2008.
4. Michael Krepon and Chris Gagne (eds.), "The Stability-Instability Paradox: Nuclear Weapons and Brinksmanship in South Asia," *Stimson Centre Report 38*, June 2001, http://beta.stimson/org/pub.cfm?id=1, accessed on 21 June 2009.
5. For a detailed recent account of "swarming" and its applicability in the modern context, see John Arquilla, "The New Rules of War," *Foreign Policy*, March/April 2010, http://www.foreignpolicy.com/articles/2010/02/22/the_new_rules_of_war, accessed on 21 June 2010.
6. Pakistan's 22 CAVALRY and 38 CAVALRY tank regiments.
7. It also captured Pt. 13,620 in the Kargil sector of J&K, a mountain-top position that overlooked Kargil town on the Srinagar-Leh road and the Indian brigade headquarters located nearby, and from where there had also been regular shelling.
8. Partly using its newly-supplied American arms and equipment, received as part of the arrangements under its joining the American-led anti-Soviet CENTO military alliance.
9. Though never on their own soil.
10. Sukhwant Singh, *India's Wars Since Independence, Vol. 3: General Trends* (New Delhi: Lancer Publishers, 1998), pp. 21-2.
11. Except in the Fazilka sector, but without any serious consequence. Here, the

defences on the Sabuna Distributory, close to the Sulaimanke Headworks on the Pakistan side, were attacked successfully by Pakistan in its effort to bolster the defence of the these canal headworks.

12. Singh, n. 10, p. 31.
13. Italicised words within brackets inserted by this author for the sake of clarity.
14. Singh, n. 10, pp. 31-2.
15. Ministry of Home Affairs, Government of India, *Annual Report, 2008-09*, p. 30. http://www.mha.nic.in/pdfs/AR(E)0809.pdf, accessed on 30 March 2009.
16. As the present LoC was known till December 1971.
17. Ministry of Home Affairs, n. 15.
18. EN Rammohan, former Director General BSF, in a talk delivered at the United Service Institution of India, on 23 October 2002.
19. Ibid.

CHAPTER 4

# India's Less-threatened Borders

## The Indo-Bangladesh Border

The Bangladesh border is another political border that divides undifferentiated territory and peoples, large stretches of difficult terrain, with pockets or "enclaves" in the "adverse possession" of each other, and is thus difficult to police. The problems here are of a localised and petty nature:

1. Illegal immigration of Bangladeshi nationals into India for better economic opportunities, smuggling, trans-border criminal and illegal activities;
2. Infiltration into India by fundamental Islamic militants and movement across the border by separatist Indian militants of the north-eastern states; and
3. Support for petty smuggling by local inhabitants of the border zone.

Unfortunately, Islamic fundamentalism is on the rise among certain segments of the Bangladesh population, often aided and abetted by Pakistan's ISI. Fundamentalist Islamists in both countries maintain close ties with each other on their common anti-India platform. As an unrelated issue, cross-border illegal immigration into India for better economic prospects continues where it can. Fortunately, due to good relations between the two governments, and the suppression of violent religious fundamentalism by the Bangladesh government, this is being kept in check to the extent possible. In addition, a recent in-principle agreement between the two governments for the establishment of local "border *haats*" (markets) is likely to reduce or even eradicate the problem of petty smuggling.

The border thus remains a problematic issue in spite of formally friendly relations between the two governments; for India mainly, due to the illegal migration of Bangladeshis into India. The designated BGF for this border is the BSF, which has 802 BOPs located along it, but in order to reduce the inter-BOP distance, 383 more BOPs have been sanctioned.[1]

*Military Requirements*

Under ordinary circumstances, this 4097 kms-long border is not under threat of armed attack or incursion by the Bangladesh Government's forces. Nevertheless, there are certain military precautions that need to be taken, in terms of contingency military planning and preparedness for some sensitive areas and locations. The first of these is the Siliguri Corridor, connecting West Bengal to Assam and the north-eastern States. This narrow corridor in the plains between Bangladesh and the mountains of Darjeeling and Sikkim to its north could be threatened by Bangladeshi military action, in collusion with China in the event of relations between India and Bangladesh souring. The aerial distance from the India-Bangladesh IB to the Sino-Indian border in Sikkim is a mere 50 kms approximately. Indian defence preparedness takes this into account by catering for adequate peace-time locations of troops to allow a quick reaction time for occupying defensive positions, if so needed, and for protection of the VAs and VPs that merit military protection. Other areas and specific sites include the Farakka Barrage on the Ganges River, which is situated close to the border in West Bengal, and the Haldia Port installations on the Bay of Bengal coast in the south. These places could be attacked in various ways by armed Islamic fundamentalist elements in times of India-Pakistan war or other tense times. In peace-time, the entire border with Bangladesh, which runs along the states of West Bengal, Assam, Meghalaya, Tripura, and Mizoram, is guarded by the BSF. No alternate military option is considered necessary at present.

*Peace-time Requirements*

This border constitutes a major peace-time problem. Though border management in peace-time is a subject dealt with by the MHA, it can pose enough of a security threat for the MoD to be involved. Key security concerns relate to the problem of uncontrolled migration, which Bangladesh refuses to recognise, across the 4,000 kms-long common boundary, the presence and activities of Indian insurgent groups and leaders from the north-east of India on Bangladeshi soil which it refuses to acknowledge, the rising influence of political parties and organisations of radical Islamic and fundamentalist orientation within and outside the coalition government led by the Bangladesh National Party,[2] and border demarcation and border management problems which give rise to ugly incidents from time to time. Border management problems, such as smuggling, illegal immigration, insurgency, trafficking of women and children, and the construction, repair and maintenance of boundary-related structures, are addressed through Border Coordination Conferences between the BSF and Bangladesh Rifles (BDR) while issues such as exchange of enclaves and adverse possessions are addressed by the Joint Boundary Working Groups (JBWGs) constituted for the purpose.[3]

Part of the problem is of India's own making. This had led the Bangladesh Government to believe that the Government of India was not serious in solving the demarcation-related problems and the issue of "adverse possession of enclaves"[4] in the spirit of the Indira Gandhi-Mujibur Rehman agreement of 1974 (the Indo-Bangladesh Agreement of 1974). The agreement was subject to ratification by the two governments. Bangladesh ratified it in November 1974. However, India has still not ratified it. The Indian government argued that ratification needed parliamentary approval, which could not be obtained until the entire border had been demarcated, and the areas to be exchanged had been identified on the ground. It has however been pointed out that under the Constitution of India, the ratification of a treaty or an agreement is an executive prerogative and no legislative approval is required.[5]

The other problem, which is an outcome of Bangladesh's over-population, is a constant population overflow outwards into less densely populated areas, in search of *lebensraum*. A significant part of this overflow is into India's north-eastern states, where the Muslim population is thus increasing at a rate greater than a normal growth rate.[6] This has, therefore, become an emotive issue with the Assamese-speaking majority Hindu population of Assam, and thus a major political issue. Pakistan's ISI supports militant Muslim groups in India's north-east for its long-term objective of destabilising India, an activity which it earlier found convenient to progress via Bangladesh.

*West Bengal:* This sector has a 2,217 kms-long border, with inadequate BSF troops to safeguard it, till a few years ago. This was in spite of the fencing that had been planned for 1376 kms then being erected. BSF battalions were looking after more than 100 kms of border each, and inter-BOP distance was five to seven kms. The area of responsibility for a battalion needed to be brought down to 30-40 kms, for only then would it have been possible for some degree of control to be achieved.[7] The problem may have eased somewhat since then, but the problems of villages being located on the Bangladesh side of the fence, and thus stuck between the fence and a foreign country, and associated issues, still remain.

*Dhubri District of Assam:* A short segment of border, 134 kms-long, but with numerous problems for the BSF. Though all but 6.1 kms of the border is fenced, the last 20 kms lie along the Brahmaputra River, which periodically changes course and washes away the fencing and the parallel border road. Both smuggling and illegal immigration are rife. On the Indian side, the villages are inhabited by immigrant Bangladeshi Muslims, inhabiting a stretch from Hallidayganj to Mancachar, and the plains area beyond to Mahendraganj and Phulbari.[8]

*Meghalaya:* The 443 kms-long border runs along the foothills of the Garo, Khasi and Jaintia Hills. In 2002, the inter-BOP distance was five to eight kms, and the sector remains difficult to manage. Large groups of Bangladeshi villagers armed with spears and *daos* intent on illegal quarrying of stone and coal, and cutting of firewood, were regularly threatening small BSF OPs and patrols, often forcing them to open fire in self-defence. These incidents led to diplomatic problems, with the Bangladesh government blaming the BSF for firing on "innocent grass-cutters". This has possibly reduced now, in the improved Indo-Bangladesh diplomatic climate. Local smuggling takes places due to the traders on both sides conniving with each other, partly due to the lack of permission for legal local cross-border trade in household requisites, but this too may abate, with this trade becoming legal. With only six BSF battalions in 2002 for the 443 kms of border, each battalion was covering up to 80 kms in difficult hilly and wooded terrain.[9]

*Cachar District of Assam:* A short 134 kms stretch of border in plain, thickly-populated agricultural country, with three BSF battalions responsible for it in 2002. The inter-BOP distance is fairly short, and each battalion's area of responsibility is manageable. The population on both sides is Bengali Muslim, and the smuggling of local necessities is a constant problem. Illegal exfiltration and infiltration by Manipuri extremist groups to and from Bangladesh takes place through the pockets of Manipuri Meitei population that exist in this area.[10]

*Tripura:* This long border of 856 kms has been a problem for the BSF to control. The main problem is to prevent armed infiltration by the secessionist aboriginal underground groups. These groups resent the huge influx of Bengali Hindus that took place after Partition, resulting in their population percentage declining from 75 percent in 1947 to 25 percent at present. These groups are being nurtured by the Bangladeshi DGFI, and use the wooded hill slopes for evading detection while crossing the border. The BSF battalions are responsible for 60 to 80 kms of border each in the best of circumstances, with an average of 100 kms per battalion, and thus cannot achieve the desirable inter-BOP distance of three kms. In the areas of difficult terrain, some of the BOPs are not connected by road, and are located at distances of three to four day's march away.[11]

*Mizoram:* This 318 kms-long border runs from the tri-junction of Tripura, Mizoram and the Chittagong Hill Tracts (CHT) of Bangladesh to another tri-junction, that of Mizoram, Bangladesh and Myanmar at Parva. In 2002, there was only one BSF battalion responsible for this entire stretch, and the inter-BOP distance was 15-20 kms. The border and its hinterland in India are both inadequately policed. The secessionist Naga organisation, the National Socialist Council of Nagaland (Isaac-Muivah group) [NSCN (IM)] has been using this area for ferrying arms. These are collected from the port of Cox's Bazar in Bangladesh and taken to Nagaland, via Mizoram and Manipur.[12]

## The Indo-Myanmar Border

This 1,643 kms-long boundary is both delimited and demarcated on the ground, with no boundary or territorial dispute between the two countries. As such, there is no military threat from the Myanmar Government. However, since the Sino-Myanmar border in northern Myanmar is at a distance that needs to be taken cognisance of, some thought needs to be given to military deployments in Upper Assam in particular. Though the likelihood of a Chinese attack through Myanmar to Upper Assam is considered a remote possibility, the capabilities of the PRC's 15$^{th}$ Airborne (AB) Army, a corps-size formation of three AB divisions, to conduct a forced insertion using one AB division into Upper Assam in conjunction with border operations, needs to be considered. The first part of this concern, that of an overland Chinese military operation through Myanmar, however remote, is apparently being taken care of. The Myanmar border as such does not require military defensive deployment planning and preparedness, which the region last witnessed during the Second World War, when the Japanese attacked India across this border.[13] However, the mountainous and mostly thickly-forested border region, through which the boundary passes can be easily crossed by armed separatist militant groups of the various ethnic separatist movements, is of concern. This factor does not constitute a military problem but rather an occasional internal security or COIN challenge to the combined security forces of the Central and concerned State Governments. Since the Central Government's "Peace Accord" with the separatist Naga movement, there has been no hostile armed activity in the State of Nagaland or in neighbouring Naga-inhabited areas of Manipur state by these armed groups. Other ethnic armed groups in Manipur have, however, remained active against both the Central and State Governments for other causes. These are primarily in the nature of law-and-order problems or low-level COIN for the State's law-enforcing machinery. Present military contingency planning and peace-time locations in this area are primarily an insurance against a serious breakdown in law and order and a resultant necessity for COIN operations. The border is safeguarded by a Central BGF, the Assam Rifles, under the "one border-one force" policy.[14] No alternate military options appear necessary.

*Peace-time Requirements*

As previously noted, this border does not pose a military problem at present. Fortunately, it does not pose much of a peace-time security problem either, in respect of the border itself. Its hinterland, however, continues to seethe with numerous unsettled socio-economic and demographic problems, resulting in multiple underground insurgent groups posing a constant problem of militancy. This affects normal civic administrative functioning and development. Both the border and the interior of the Indo-Myanmar border states are the responsibility of the Assam Rifles (AR), under the 'one border-one force' principle. The AR is unique among the BGFs, in that it has a very significant mandated COIN role as well, and is structured for COIN operations within its designated north-eastern India area of responsibility. It has been officered by Army officers from pre-Independence days. The AR are the most military in ethos and functioning and the force has been successfully used for COIN operations even outside the north-east. Its border-guarding responsibility used to include the entire Sino-Indian frontier in eastern India, starting from Sikkim and going eastwards to the Tibet-India-Myanmar tri-junction (excluding the Bhutan-Tibet border). In some areas, it operates directly under the Army's control for COIN operations. Elsewhere, it functions partly under the civil administration of the concerned State and partly through its own administrative channels. This administrative arrangement is not the best possible arrangement, either for the Indo-Tibet border, or for the interior areas of the states bordering Myanmar.

The role and tasks of the Assam Rifles have been spelt out as under:

- Conduct COIN operations in the north-east and other areas where deemed necessary, under control of the Army;
- During peace and "proxy" war, ensure security of the Sino-Indian and Indo-Myanmar borders;
- During war, ensure rear area security in the tactical battle area;
- Act as the penultimate interventionist force of the Central Government in internal security situations, under the control of the Army, when the situation goes beyond the control of the Central para-military organisations.[15]

The AR has prided itself on being known as "the friends of the hill people", as they had been described by Verrier Elwin, and had till fairly recent times, been well-regarded by the locals of all the various ethnic communities in the north-eastern hill regions. In pre-Independence days, when there were only six battalions, the composition of its soldiers was only Gorkhas,[16] and the officers on deputation to the force were only from Gorkha regular infantry regiments of the Indian Army. The various AR battalions were affiliated to various Gorkha Rifles (GR) regiments, which provided the deputationist officers. With the onset of the Naga insurrection in the 1950s, numerous more AR battalions were raised, and the class composition of its solders broadened, to include Kumaonis and Garhwalis as well, plus a reservation for a maximum of ten percent locals, i.e. Assamese, Nagas, Mizos and Kukis, and the other smaller communities. Thus, a sort of "all-hillmen" character was preserved in the AR, and the soldiers had a certain degree of empathy with the locals, and sympathy for their hard lives, which they well understood. Intelligence networks were easily established even where there was an influential presence of "underground hostiles". The local people did not overly resent the AR presence, which also often provided the only available medical and emergency hospital facilities. The inconveniences of cordon and search operations were forgiven, and ambushes by either side were understood as each others' "duties", with wounds or death as the honorable chances of war. Rapes by soldiers were unheard of, but there were often cases of soldiers marrying local girls, without any hostility from the local community.[17]

With an overall deterioration in the internal security situation in the north-eastern states, and the necessity of increasing the availability of CPMF, the AR was expanded greatly. A concomitant necessity perhaps was the change in MHA policy, which dictated that the AR should have an "all-India" character with its soldiers being drawn from all over India, as in the BSF or the CRPF. The ten percent reservation for locals was retained, but the troops were no longer "all hill-men" from the Himalayan states and Nepal. The softer inter-personal relationship style of such troops had endeared them to the local populations, who saw them as basically gentle enforcers of the law and of the writ of the state. The change in the class composition to "All Indian Classes" also resulted in a difference in the functional attitudes and behavior of the AR's soldiers, to somewhat harsher, less empathic behavior and inter-personal dealings with the local populace. Part of this change was the difference in the cultural attitude to the local women, from the easier acceptance of local cultures to a sometimes more sexually predatory attitude based on a misunderstanding of social norms. This resulted in a gradual change in the attitude of the local population to the AR, which slowly began to be seen by some local populations as something in the nature of an unwanted "occupying force", just as the CRPF, BSF and Indian Army are viewed by the locals in the Kashmir Valley. A lack of friendliness in the attitude of the locals also led to a harder attitude on the part of the AR's troops in some cases. The cases of July 1987, and 12 February 1998, and the unwarranted use of force case of November 2000, can be seen to be an unintended fallout-out of the present manning policy.[18] The agitation in Manipur for the repeal of the Armed Forces (Special Powers) Act, 1958 (AFSPA), is a direct outcome. The AFSPA is not a defective act, and is necessary for the effective prosecution of COIN operations. However, its use has to be made with necessary fair-mindedness as it is being used against the country's own citizens. Good-quality officers and subordinate officers are important, and the attitudes of the soldiers prevent atrocities and other misuse of the powers granted by it.

## The Indo-Nepal Border

This 1,751 kms-long border is not disputed, except in one minor area, which is more an issue of demarcation than of territorial dispute. Over most of its length, it has been delimited and 98 percent of it is demarcated. Fortunately, due to the nature of the generally cordial relations between the governments and the peoples of both countries, it does not constitute a source of much friction. There is no appreciable direct military threat to Indian territory from the organs of the Nepal Government, and, as such, no assessed need for military planning and preparedness to defend this boundary or the border zone militarily. There are two factors which have a military bearing in connection with this border. The first is the unlikely possibility of Chinese forces from across the Nepal-Tibet border moving through Nepal, and posing a military threat to the densely-populated heart of the Indo-Gangetic plains of northern India. The second are two potential threats to internal security: (1) In the event of an Indo-Pakistan war, by militant Islamic fundamentalists sent into Nepal by Pakistan's ISI, who can easily cross this porous border; (2) Armed assistance to leftist extremists of the Communist Part of India (Maoist) [CPI(Maoist)] by renegade underground elements of Nepal's Maoist People's Liberation Army. Neither of these potential threats to India's security constitutes a threat to India's territorial integrity and thus, do not warrant military contingency planning. This border is looked after by a Central BGF, the SSB.

### *Peace-time Requirements*

Formerly a peaceful and unthreatened border covered by only routine civil policing and some Central Government counter-intelligence surveillance, two disparate socio-political developments have altered its importance. Both of these pose considerable internal security risk, as noted earlier in the military consideration of this border. One is the presence of a large Maoist Naxalite left-wing extremist organisation with great influence in the hills of the lower and middle Himalayas, in Nepal beyond the Terai. The other is a dramatic rise in the number of *madrassas* on both sides of the border in the lowland agricultural Terai area through which the IB runs. Both diplomatic influence on Nepal and active policing are necessary here. Since June 2001, this 1,751 kms-long border is the responsibility of the SSB, which is also the Lead Intelligence Agency (LIA) for this border and the Indo-Bhutan border. In 2008-9, a total strength of 27 battalions was available for the 1,751 kms length of the Nepal and the 699 kms of the Bhutan border. 450 BOPs were sanctioned for the Nepal border, with 436 established by 2008-9.[19] However, the planned additional raisings of about 16 more SSB battalions would allow both borders to be more effectively policed as intended.

*Intelligence Requirement for States Bordering Nepal:* Four Indian states border Nepal: West Bengal with 105.6 kms of common border, Bihar with 800.4 kms, Uttar Pradesh with 599.3 kms, and Uttarakhand with 263.7 kms. As the LIA for the border, the SSB has a big task on its hands in dealing with the following two issues.

(1) *The Madrassa Phenomenon:* The Terai zone on both sides of the border is inhabited by Hindustani-speaking people in the States of Bihar and Uttar Pradesh through which it runs. There are people of both Hindu and Muslim faiths on both sides. It is believed that the sudden increase in the number of *madrassas* has come about due to an influx of foreign money. This is believed to be mainly from Saudi Arabia, both directly to Muslim socio-religious groups, and also channeled through Pakistan, whose nationals can easily cross this under-policed border. These *madrassas* make collections from the local Muslims, and collect from Muslims in towns and cities near and far. These cash donations cannot explain the large buildings and other infrastructure which even seemingly poor local *masjids* have managed. For poor Muslim families in under-developed backward areas, the opportunity to send a son or two to an institution with free food and lodging, and eventually the possibility of a livelihood as a religious teacher, is a big attraction. Recent arrests have indicated the degree of active interest the Pakistani ISI and other non-state fundamentalist organisations are taking in this border zone.

(2) *The Maoist Link to India's 'Red Corridor':* This area is geographically the link zone between the India's Naxalite Maoists and Nepal's Maoists, and thus needs close watch.

## The Indo-Bhutan Border

This relatively short 700 kms-long border is not militarily threatened, and has the least internal security implications at present. The two governments have good relations and cooperate on security issues. The Royal Bhutan Army had mounted operations against Bodo and United Liberation Front of Asom (ULFA) militants who had established camps in the forests on the Bhutanese side of the border. With these elements pushed back into India, the border itself is not threatened in any way. The Indian Army has in the past mounted

COIN operations against Bodo and ULFA militants when requested by the Assam Government, as aid to the civil authority. Both "Operation BAJRANG" and "Operation RHINO" were successful in stabilising the internal security situation in Assam.

*Peace-time Requirements*

This 699 kms portion of India's land frontiers is at neither serious nor constant risk. Cordial relations with the Bhutan government allow this border to be kept mainly under low-key policing. The BGF responsible for this border is the SSB, which is also responsible for the Indo-Nepal border. There are 132 BOPs sanctioned for this IB, with 127 having been established by 2008-9.[20] Four states share borders with Bhutan: Arunachal Pradesh with a 217 kms-long common border, Assam with 267 kms, West Bengal with 183 kms, and Sikkim with 32 kms.

It can be seen from this survey of India's land borders in the last three chapters that the basic military requirements as well as the peace-time border securing and policing requirements have been examined and mostly addressed, or are in the process of being catered to. Nevertheless, the fundamental premise on which these arrangements have been made is that of a fairly limited threat from across the various borders. They are also based on an entirely defensive policy of halting and repelling from own territory any military ground attack, which is not linked to any stated retaliatory policy. On the overall plane, it can be said that a purely defensive policy, with or without a counter-offensive capability and policy, should cater to the large numbers of available reserve defensive forces, organised into capable military fighting formations. Without sufficient numbers of these, the ability to prosecute a defensive military campaign to a satisfactory conclusion will be severely constrained.

## NOTES

1. Ministry of Home Affairs, Government of India, *Annual Report, 2008-09*, p. 30. http://www.mha.nic.in/pdfs/AR(E)0809.pdf, accessed on 30 March 2009.
2. Though this is no longer the case, with the democratic change of government there.
3. Ministry of Defence, "National Security Environment: An Overview," http://mod.nic.in/aforces/welcome.html, accessed on 30 July 2009.
4. There are 111 Indian enclaves within Bangladesh in the border zone, totalling 17,000 acres of land, and 51 Bangladeshi enclaves within India totalling 7,000 acres.

5. NS Jamwal, "Border Management: Dilemma of Guarding the India-Bangladesh Border," *Strategic Analysis*, Vol. 28. No. 1, January-March 2004, pp. 7-8.
6. See Rohit Srivastava, "Unwelcome Immigrants: A Security Threat," *Defence and Security Alert*, Vol. 1, No. 5, February 2010, pp. 51-55, and "20 million illegal immigrants in India," *Assam Tribune,* 14 May 2010.
7. EN Rammohan, former Director General BSF, in a talk delivered at the United Service Institution of India, on 23 October 2002.
8. Ibid.
9. Ibid.
10. Ibid.
11. Ibid.
12. Ibid.
13. The last time a military attack was launched across this border onto Indian territory was in 1944, during the Second World War. Japan's Burma Area Army, under Lt Gen Masakazu Kawabe, launched the Japanese 15th Army (the equivalent of an Indian Army Corps), commanded by Lt Gen Renya Mutaguchi, to capture the Indian towns of Imphal (Manipur) and Kohima (Nagaland). The Japanese offensive 'Operation U-GO' was aimed at securing the western flank of Myanmar, in order to turn the entire Myanmar into 'the western wall' protecting the Japanese conquest of South-east Asia. The 15th Army's 33rd Infantry Division and 15th Infantry Division were tasked to capture Imphal, while the 31st Infantry Division was to capture Kohima as a subsidiary operation. The 31st Division's attack penetrated right into the heart of Kohima town, where it was finally stopped in a desperate defence by British and some Indian troops under the British 2nd Infantry Division. Imphal was defended by the Indian 4 Corps, with mainly Indian and some British troops, consisting of three Indian infantry divisions: 17 Division (of only two brigades), 20 Division, and 23 Division (severely under-strength), plus 254 Indian Tank Brigade and 50 Indian Parachute Brigade. The determined Japanese attack eventually failed, greatly due to poor logistical support and non-existent medical cover. The Japanese suffered 53,879 battle casualties in the Kohima and Imphal battles, including13,500 killed. Indian and British killed and wounded totaled 17,500.
14. Group of Ministers' Report, "Reforming the National Security System," *Ministry of Defence*, 26 February 2001, para no. 5.12.
15. "Role and Tasks," *Assam Rifles—Friends of the Hill People*, www.assamrifles.com and www.assamrifles.gov.in, accessed on 21 June 2009.
16. Gorkhas, other than the Rajput-descended Khas and Thakur Gorkhas, speak Tibeto-Burman "home" languages themselves, such as Magarkura, Gurungkura, and Limbukura, for example, and thus find it easy to pick up the local Tibeto-Burman languages and dialects. The "Gorkhali" or "Nepali" spoken in Gorkha units is an Indo-Sanskritic language, and the *lingua franca* and official language of Nepal, used as a common regimental language.
17. From personal knowledge. This author has been on deputation to the AR in the 1970s. He served in a battalion and actively participated in COIN operations in Nagaland before the Shillong "Peace Accord" of 1975 came into effect. In an AR

battalion, he has been, in turn, a Sub-Wing Commander commanding the equivalent of a regular infantry company, Adjutant of the 1,450 man battalion, and a Wing Commander commanding about 360 men. In addition to active COIN operations, his battalion's responsibilities included protection of one part of the Indo-Myanmar border. AR battalions have since been re-organised and now comprise six rifle companies and a Battalion HQ.

18. All these three incidents took place in Manipur.
19. Ministry of Home Affairs, Government of India, *Annual Report, 2008-09*, p. 32, http://www.mha.nic.in/pdfs/AR(E)0809.pdf, accessed on 30 March 2009.
20. Ibid., p. 33.

# CHAPTER 5

# India's Maritime Borders

## India's Coastal Security Requirements

India's 7,516.6 kms-long coastline,[1] of which 5,700 kms is on the Indian mainland, had been a vulnerable area ever since Independence and the withdrawal of Britain's Royal Navy from the Indian Ocean region. Coastal security had been a neglected area until the country was rudely awakened by the well-planned Mumbai terror attack of 26 November 2008. Numerous short-comings in India's security arrangements and responses were clearly brought out, in full public gaze. As far as coastal security measures go, "26/11", as the marine commando-style terrorist raid from the sea has come to be known, is the coastal version of Kargil 1999. In the aftermath, the Government's decision to make the Indian Navy the nodal agency responsible for coastal protection has come better late than never. While seaward defence and coastal protection are two different kettles of fish altogether, the responsibility becoming that of the armed forces' maritime arm will undoubtedly bring a greater professionalism and a Central Government over-watch to a neglected field. The national laxity on the subject was carefully studied by an inimical terrorist organisation which took brazen advantage of it. India had created a Central security organisation for taking care of this aspect quite some time ago, but its organisation, equipment, and functional ethos had evidently not been thought through well enough. The Coast Guard, set up on 01 February 1977 under the Ministry of Defence as the fourth of India's armed forces, is the only one of these whose primary function lies in its peace-time role. It therefore needs to guard against acquiring a more relaxed functional attitude than the Navy. A closer Navy-Coast Guard synergy will no doubt ensure better inshore security for India. In fact, it is so important that the ideal staffing method for the Coast Guard would have been to have all its sailors and officers on deputation from the Navy, thus completely eliminating any "separate ethos" situation.

Securing a notional International Maritime Boundary Line (IMBL) against unauthorised entry is not an easy matter in the practical sphere. For example, the RDX used in the 1993 Mumbai bombings was smuggled in through the Kutch coast. Following this incident, "Operation SWAN" was launched to check infiltration into the Gujarat and Maharashtra coasts. As part of this, three-layered patrolling was to be carried out between the IMBL and the Gujarat coast. The Navy and the Coast Guard were to patrol the high seas and the intermediate waters, while inshore waters were to jointly patrolled by the Navy, Coast Guard, Customs and State Police. Later, an all-India "Coastal Security Scheme" had been initiated in 2005 and launched in 2006. This had sanctioned 73 Coastal Police Stations, 97 Check Posts, 58 Outposts and 30 operational barracks. Its lack of success as a regular measure has been proved by the 26 November 2008 Mumbai terrorist attack, wherein the Pakistani terrorists used a small motor vessel to reach the coast off Bombay. The Coastal Security Scheme has not made much headway against the opposing headwinds and high seas of State governments' indifference. Nor has the plan for setting up a Coastal Security Police Force (CSPF) jointly implemented by the MHA and the MoD, intended to be completed by 2012, had smooth sailing. The plan for Gujarat, for example, envisaged the establishment of 10 coastal police stations, 30 vessels, and associated infrastructure. This force was supposed to be the first line of seaward defence, and to be responsible out to five nautical miles (9.3 kms) from shore. It was to coordinate and jointly operate with the Coast Guard, Customs, individual port managements, and the Navy, and any other agencies involved. It is floundering in the Gujarat government's apathy. Meanwhile, the stretch of about 80 kms between Medhi and Jakhau, which is not covered either by the BSF or by the Coast Guard, remains unsecured. The last BSF BOP on the landward side is at Medhi while the Coast Guard station is at Jakhau.

Port security of the numerous minor ports is another cause for concern. While designated "major ports" are authorised Central Industrial Security Force (CISF) protection, the minor ports employ only private security firms, whose personnel are not legally empowered to carry or use fire-arms. The sea off most Indian ports is not covered by any Vessel Traffic Management System (VTMS) which would allow the checking and regulation of marine traffic. Thus, though the 2001 GoM Report on National Security had advocated the tightening-up of coastal security, there is still a long way to go before all becomes smooth sailing on this subject.[2]

While the professionals of maritime security in both the armed maritime forces are working towards improving this through acquisition of more of the right kind of equipment, it might not be out of place to share a thought on this subject. From the recent news reports[3] and from the Coast Guard's own website,[4] it appears that, even with the planned acquisitions of fast, shallow draft inshore patrol vessels and interceptor boats, the coast will still require more surveillance effort. Aerial surveillance appears to be an area which will need more emphasis, with slow-flying fixed-wing aircraft of maximum endurance being the equipment of choice. If such Maritime Reconnaissance (MR) aircraft can have some fitted armament, such as medium machine guns and a fast-firing cannon, it would be a potent platform indeed, and a strong deterrent to small craft attempting to sneak in. It is worth considering such an aircraft with sea-landing and take-off capability, such as the Shin-Meiwa PS-1 flying-boats operated till 1989 by Japan's Maritime Self-Defence Force, and China's Harbin SH-5 which is still in service. A smaller and yet-versatile modern flying boat, though not originally designed for military duties, is the smaller twin-turboprop Canadian CL-215 and its military variant, the Bombardier 415. It is also worth considering lighter and cheaper twin-turboprop float planes (high-wing aircraft fitted with twin pontoons to enable water landing and take-off) as shorter-range MR aircraft. Such designs as a modernised version of the old De Havilland Canada DHC-6 Twin Otter in its float plane configuration would be ideal, but there are many rugged modern easy-to-maintain bush planes with floats that could do the job. This inshore MR requirement is a purely Coast Guard requirement and it is suggested that their aviation wing consider such aircraft for their inventory.

## NOTES

1. Ministry of Home Affairs, Government of India, *Annual Report, 2008-09*, p. 24, http://www.mha.nic.in/pdfs/AR(E)0809.pdf, accessed on 30 March 2009.
2. Interaction with Pushpita Das, Associate Fellow, Institute for Defence Studies and Analyses, 29 April 2009.
3. Shishir Gupta, "After the disaster, Navy, Coast Guard operation rooms to be linked," *Indian Express*, 04 January 2009, http://www.indianexpress.com/news/after-the-disaster-navy-coast-guard-operation-rooms-to-be-linked/406388/, accessed on 30 May 2009.
4. "Indian Coast Guard," www.indiancoastguard.nic.in, accessed on 30 July 2009.

# Part II
# FORCES

CHAPTER 6

# The Army's Role and Budgetary Allocations

In theory, any small or medium-sized country can be defended by positioning a modern army of adequate size and capability somewhere in the centre of the country, to react, both offensively across its borders, or defensively within its borders, as decided by the national leadership. It is possible some such policy would have been decided upon for a newly-independent India, had the J&K operations of 1947-49 not begun soon after Independence, resulting in a "tight defence" of the Indo-Pakistan frontiers, particularly in the west.[1] Ever since then, the residents of the areas bordering Pakistan, in particular, have an inherent sense of insecurity, which can only be allayed by an effective system of border guarding in peacetime and border defence in war. In a democratic country, therefore, it is a political imperative that "no loss of territory" becomes a military term of reference where defence of the country's territorial integrity is concerned. The border war with the PRC in the Himalayan region in 1962 resulted in a change in the national mindset regarding the hitherto traditionally peaceful pre-1962 Indo-Tibetan border. Thus, the system of securing India's Indo-Pakistan and Indo-Tibetan borders has moved permanently away from theoretical models of national defence such as "mobile war" to a politically-mandated "border defence" system.

The historic evolution since Independence in 1947 towards a "fortress" system of defence planning envisaging well-defended borders is a new development for India. Unlike the case in Imperial China, for example, which has had such a policy for over a thousand years, the historical tradition in India had been for fortified cities and even villages, but not that of a fortified country. This was primarily because there had been no indigenous sense of being one political India, except when the different regions and areas had been politically united under an empire, the last being that of the British up to August 1947. The historical and strategic developments on and across India's borders since 1947 have imposed a military defensive policy and system which now functions on the underlying policy basis of a fortified and defensible border.[2] However, the "Fortress India" border defence policy has been in development, both in theory and practice, for a relatively short period, only about three decades. Much of the practical aspects have been reactionary, though some have been evolutionary. A holistic examination such as this needs to study both streams of development of the present system, so that realistic recommendations for improvement can be arrived at.

## India's Borders

India shares borders with four other countries of the Indian sub-continent, with the Central Asian regions of Sinkiang (Xinjiang) and Tibet of the PRC, and with the South-East Asian country of Myanmar (formerly known as Burma). It also has a *de jure* border with another South Asian country, Afghanistan, though this is presently along the Pakistan-occupied part of the state of J&K, no longer physically in Indian-controlled territory, and is disputed by Pakistan. India's claimed land border, including the total length of the boundaries of Indian enclaves, is approximately 15,200 kms-long. India's maritime boundaries extend along its 7,683 kms-long coastline and around its island territories in the Bay of Bengal and the Arabian Sea. However, the physical boundary on the ground includes various less-well defined or disputed alignments, in addition to a mutually-recognised International Boundary (IB). These are the militarily active Line of Control (LoC)[9] and Actual Ground Position Line (AGPL) with Pakistan Occupied Kashmir (POK) in J&K, and an un-delimited Line of Actual Control (LAC) with the PRC in two large parts of the Sino-Indian border.

The IB with Bangladesh has a few un-demarcated riverine stretches and some pockets of land (called "enclaves") which are physically surrounded by the other country, thus causing day-to-day friction. The LoC and the AGPL in J&K are being militarily defended *in situ* by the Army, as there continues to be a real danger of the Pakistan Army occupying further territory if these are not physically held. The LAC, which is supposedly the current physical boundary between the territory of the PRC and that of India, is usually not threatened with physical encroachment in most areas, thanks to a stand-still diplomatic arrangement. It is, however, not mutually agreed upon yet as an IB, in the legal and diplomatic sense. What many choose to call a Sino-Indian "border dispute" or "boundary dispute" is actually so only in the Himachal Pradesh and Uttarakhand Sectors. In the J&K and in the Arunachal Pradesh Sectors, it is actually a serious territorial dispute, a major disease of which the "boundary issue" is only a symptom. The MoD describes the Sino-Indian border thus:

> India's border with China is almost 3,500 kms-long. China continues to occupy approx. 38,000 sq kms of Indian territory, mainly in the Aksai Chin Area, and claims yet another 90,000 sq kms in the Eastern Sector. Further, 5,180 sq kms of territory under Pak occupation in Northern Kashmir was illegally ceded to China by Pakistan in 1963. (Whilst several rounds of Border Talks have been held with China, a number of disputed pockets remain).[3]

India's actual land borders with its neighbours, as per the Ministry of Defence,[4] are as under:

- Myanmar - 1,643 kms
- China - 4,056 kms (about 3,460 kms along the LAC)[5]
- Bangladesh - 4,351 kms (4,096.7 kms excluding the peripheries of enclaves within Bangladesh)
- Bhutan - 699 kms
- Nepal - 1,751 kms
- Pakistan - 3,244 kms (3,323 kms as per the MHA)[6]

## Historical Evolution of the Border Security System

Today's border defence and border security policies and practices have been put in place due to practical necessity at different times since Independence. They can thus be considered to be evolutionary rather than the result of fresh thinking starting from a clean slate. To place the current border defence thought-process and the border security mechanism in perspective, it is necessary to briefly examine their historical evolution.

India's present system of defending its territorial integrity has evolved mainly from expedients adopted out of urgent necessity in the first 18 years of its existence as an independent country. The Kashmir war of 1947-49, the Sino-Indian border war of October-November 1962, the Pakistani attack on Kutch in April 1965 and the India-Pakistan war of September 1965, as also the Siachen Glacier operations of 1984, have all contributed both to the present border defence posture and the current policy regarding the security of the Pakistan and China borders. Security policies and postures for the

Bangladesh, Myanmar, Nepal and Bhutan borders have evolved gradually, from political developments in both India and the neighbouring country concerned.

From soon after Independence on 15 August 1947, India was involved in the military defence of the borders of the erstwhile princely state of J&K, which had just acceded to the Indian Union. The invasion of Pathan tribals, abetted and aided by the Pakistan Government, which began on 22 October 1947, resulted in the first India-Pakistan war over Kashmir. The eventual cessation of hostilities left a permanent defensive military deployment in the state, in the form of fixed defences along what became known as the Cease-Fire Line (CFL). The present military deployment along the LoC, the current name for the CFL, adopted after the December 1971 India-Pakistan war, is by and large organised on the same lines as stabilised between 1949 and 1965. The Siachen Glacier operations of 1984 ("Operation MEGHDOOT") and thereafter, have resulted in the present deployment pattern and the policy for securing the AGPL.

The Indian pattern of military deployment for the protection of the *de facto* Sino-Indian border is essentially that which resulted from the 1962 war. Treaties with China since then, concluded in 1993 and 1996, have not resulted in any substantial changes to either policy or practice. In effect, therefore, all the threatened borders, whether actively threatened or potentially threatened, are secured by a defensive system that is a product of a historical evolutionary process. Unless there are dramatic changes in the geo-political circumstances that affect India-Pakistan and India-China relations, India is trapped in a system that is not easily amenable to change or significant modification. Resistance to even logically desirable changes can be expected from: (1) The natural inertia that afflicts large organisations, more so when they have to adjust with each other; and (2) The organisational tendencies to protect one's own turf at all costs.

Just as the operational defensive policy for the Indo-Pakistan IB in the Punjab is a legacy of the 1965 war, in some respects, the existing military defensive policy and posture along the other militarily worrisome borders is also a continuing legacy of the past. The deployment and operational policies along the LoC in J&K are a legacy of the 1947-49, 1965 and 1971 wars. The deployment and tactical policies along the LAC with the PRC are based on the events of the 1962 war, with modifications brought about by incidents such as the Wangdung/Sumdorong Chu face-off of 1986-87 in Arunachal Pradesh. Many of the thought-processes that contributed to both the operational policy of deployments in peace and war continue to be valid even today, in respect of India's borders with Pakistan and the PRC. Any fresh thinking on the subject thus needs to take the logic of the existing system into account. However, every system needs periodic review, and thus, the developments of the decade between July 1999 and 2009 necessitate a re-examination. But what are the options for systemic changes that might be better than the present arrangements? For this, one will first need to look at a totality of options.

## Military Protection Options for the Borders

It is possible for a country to follow one or more of different organisational methods of securing its borders. Broadly, such policies can be segregated as under:

1. An aggressively "forward policy" that militarily engages the threatening neighbour with an attack onto his soil, before he can attack one's own border: The British Indian Empire actively pursued this policy against Afghanistan in the $19^{th}$ century and early $20^{th}$ century.[7] The PRC has implied such a policy in its current military doctrine, which includes a deterrent nuclear arsenal. This policy allows the country to maintain concentrated military forces in the rear areas, with easy access to the threatened sectors and to the hostile neighbour's vulnerable areas. Such a policy allows the country to protect its border, with a minimal deployment of BGF or even mere border police. Chinese deployment on most of its borders follows this pattern, in keeping with China's current policy of "Active Defence", which includes pre-emptive attacks across its borders.
2. An even more aggressive forward "expeditionary" policy that mandates creating a military threat-in-being to any country, neighbouring or overseas, that might pose a threat to either to the country's borders or to its interests anywhere abroad: It requires an aggressive foreign policy that does not hesitate to use force in the pursuit of its own interests, and also requires that all other countries believe that such force will be used. Such a policy was followed by most European powers in the colonial era, and is presently being followed by the US. It requires the creation of large and very powerful

armed forces with state-of-the-art armaments and equipment. It also requires the organisation of its military forces; land, sea, and air, for operations far away from the country's borders, to fight wars on the soil of distant countries. Thereby the actual borders could be merely kept under surveillance by para-military or police forces, while some reserve military organisations would be kept available for "homeland defence", if required.

3. A policy of peace treaties and active economic co-operation and trade with its neighbors, backed up by a minimal inescapable size of armed forces for unforeseen eventualities: Such forces would need to be kept at the highest level of modern armament capability, and in a reasonably high state of readiness and training. This form of border security is cheaper to maintain than either of the first two options, but requires a high level of faith and mutual trust with its neighbours. It is the system being followed by most European countries today.
4. A policy that poses a credible threat of massive retaliation, using both nuclear ballistic missiles and conventional offensive air assets, as well as conventional land forces and sea-borne forces, in case a neighbour attacks across one's borders: Pakistan attempts to use such a policy against India, even though it requires the creation and maintenance of large and capable armed forces. In Pakistan's case, the retaliatory threat is primarily by the development of a deterrent nuclear capability. The credibility of the threat is maintained by a foreign policy that stresses its low nuclear threshold, if invaded. The greater the credibility of the retaliatory threat, the less the country has to spend on or worry about the security of its borders, which can be adequately secured by small BGF.
5. A purely defensive policy of deploying ground troops to protect the borders, not credibly backed by any aggressively retaliatory foreign policy: India appears to be following this option. The military retaliatory options are seemingly kept limited to counter-air operations by the air force and some naval actions. In addition, large and capable mechanised forces are maintained for a land offensive against a neighbor in suitable plains terrain. However, the historical record from 1947 to 2010 indicates that India does not have the aggressiveness to undertake cross-border land operations even when its borders have been transgressed.[8]

While it is not practical for India to pursue Options 2 or 3 above, variations of Options 1 and 4 with respect to Pakistan and China are certainly possible for India to adopt. It primarily requires a change in attitudes, and a corresponding re-orientation of both foreign and military policies. Some of these possibilities are examined hereafter, taken sector-wise. With regard to India's borders with Bangladesh, Myanmar, Nepal, and Bhutan, where the anticipated threat is presently not that of a military aggression, better variations of India's present practices are possible, within the existing policy.

## National Defence Mindset and Policy

India's defence preparations and its responses in the modern period since August 1947 are indicative of a purely defensive policy under most circumstances, as in Option 5 above. It has been argued by Harjeet Singh that India's defensive mind-set is a cultural outcome of the geography of the Indian sub-continent.[9] The sub-continent's northern half is physically surrounded by high mountains on the east, north and north-west, while on the west, it has an inhospitable desert separating it from Iran. Central and southern India, which constitute the southern half, are surrounded by seas which in ancient times protected the coast from any major sea-borne invasion. Thus, the well-watered and fertile plains of the northern part of this sub-continent are protected by 'walls' of inhospitable geographic terrain, and the central and southern parts by an extensive moat. The basic premise is that because of these natural barriers, the cultural mindset is insular and inward-looking, and the overall defensive strategy is merely to keep intruders out. As a result, Indians historically have been content to fight defensive battles aimed at pushing intruders back, rather than aggressively destroying outside forces which had ingressed. The same culturally-determined broadly defensive strategy has rarely allowed Indians from thinking of or pursuing expeditionary strategies of attacking potential invaders outside the sub-continent, before they debouched onto the plains of northern and western India.

The armies of agricultural countries such as China and India have naturally been primarily composed of peasant-soldiers, and thus have had culturally different concepts of war than those of nomadic pastoralists, such as the Central Asian Mongols and Turkomans. Peasant armies have historically had a defensive mindset and tended to fight defensive battles from fixed defences, aimed at keeping attackers out and pushing them back. The peoples of the Indian sub-continent are thus culturally predisposed towards a "fortress mentality" due to the influence of both factors: geographical and societal. This is in contrast to the wide-ranging and fluid mobile warfare favoured by the horse-based armies of the Central Asian nomadic societies in the medieval era. It is thus easy to understand the basic Indian mindset when it comes to "defence" as a concept. Expeditionary warfare to tackle potential aggressors away from the home territory, as espoused in contemporary times by the US, for example, does not come naturally to the Indian mind for these long-established cultural reasons. Consequently, India's national policy-making on defence has been essentially defensive in nature, and "defence of national territory" has been made the Army's primary task. Basic military policy has, therefore, been primarily of the "rush to defend the border" variety, as soon as there is a perceived danger of war, in marked contrast to those of many other countries. This continues to remain a basic premise. To some observers, such as Pravin Sawhney and Ghazala Wahab, the developments since the 1998 nuclear tests have further brought about a "Fortress India" mentality, and gradually pushed India's strategic mindset, against Pakistan in particular, into a strategy of "all defence and no offence".[10] This fundamental mentality has also contributed to the decision to fence the entire Indo-Pakistan IB and the LoC in J&K, as well as the Indo-Bangladesh border.

To the lay person in India and even to very many policy-makers, the subject of "defence" and the related ones of "national security" and "military security" imply only the defence by military means of India's land borders. Thus, both to the uninformed public and to most others holding either government or public office, the safeguarding of India's territorial integrity appears to boil down to "border defence" or "border security". Though this is an over-simplistic and incomplete picture of the Army's responsibilities based on lack of knowledge, it is nevertheless the public perception. In a democratic country ruled by an elected political party, whose only authority is the public mandate, the public perception tends to become an over-riding political consideration. This, therefore, creates what amounts to a term of reference for the basic military planning process, and tends to influence the methods that could be used for defending territorial integrity.

Maintaining public morale as well as patriotic public support for the armed forces constitute important elements of a country's will to fight and win. These considerations are an additional factor in the formulation of defence policy. Military policies to which the public can relate in a patriotic sense are useful for generating the necessary public support for the Army in peace and war.

Additionally, any military policy that can harness the people's patriotism and willingness to fight for their own home area would generate a much greater overall morale and fighting spirit than would be possible from within a purely professional army.

## The Army's Role: Perceptions and Realities

*The Defined Role of the Army*

"The role of a nation's army flows from its national interests, foreign policy objectives and the national security strategy. A nation's strategic culture is also instrumental in guiding its grand strategy. Nations with a pro-active strategic culture maintain large expeditionary forces to fight and win their wars away from their homelands... India has always been inward-looking and its strategic culture, based on its civilisational values of *Ahimsa* or non-violence, non-aggressive and peaceful co-existence, tends to be reactive rather than pro-active."[11] Whether or not one agrees with the author of the quote, India's MoD has listed border defence first amongst its national security objectives, in these words: "Defending the country's borders as defined by law and enshrined in the Constitution and protecting the lives of its citizens against terrorism and insurgencies."[12] The MoD also categorically states that "The primary role of the army is to safeguard the territorial integrity of the nation against external threats," and "The basic responsibility of the Army is to safeguard the territorial integrity of the nation against external aggression."[13]

*Future War will not Necessarily be a "Border War"*

In spite of the defined role of the Army implying "border defence", in the present age, even local limited wars are likely to be short-duration, high-intensity and high-technology (hi-tech) wars. Even so-called "border wars", such as the one of the last decade (Kargil 1999), are likely to see both "unconventional" as well as "conventional" attacks on rear areas and on both civil and military infrastructure. This could be so whether the war is fought against China or Pakistan, or even both simultaneously. Current Chinese and Pakistani policies are explicit in this regard. Targets of attack would include infrastructure of surface communications or of electronic communications, as well as military C4ISR (Command, Control, Communications, Computers, Intelligence, Surveillance and Reconnaissance) systems. Since all these would be aimed at psychological dislocation and demoralising of the adversary, it would be a moot point whether any future war, even of limited aim, scope and duration, can be pre-classified as a "border war". Nevertheless, defending the border itself will continue to be a military war-fighting requirement.

*"Border Defence" and "Border Security"*

"Border Defence" being a broad generic task given to the Army, it needs to be separated into:

- Defence of the border zone in the event of war, or "Tactical and Operational Border Defence", and
- "Border Security" in times of peace, where it has been made so responsible in conjunction with other organs of the Central and State Governments that have related responsibilities.

The term "Border Management", which will also be discussed, is a wider responsibility than "Border Security", and forms a part of the broader peace-time requirement. It includes a number of non-military administrative issues which are not normally undertaken by the Indian Army, or even by India's Ministry of Defence. Since all these responsibilities are already being shouldered by various armed and civilian organs of the Government of India, including the Army, and by the affected State Governments, it is necessary to understand how the present system is expected to function.

*Defending the Border in War*

Since "defending the borders" has been made the first responsibility of the armed forces, the government will have to plan to fight right from the border, back into the depth areas within the country. Trading space to enable mobile warfare within Indian territory is not a politically feasible option, as has already been brought out. The practical implications of such a task for the army include the planning and preparations for successive "layers" of defensive battle. It also necessitates the division of the Indian frontier regions into different outward-facing lateral "zones". These lateral "zones" will require to be protected in different ways under separate conditions, such as during peace-time, in a precautionary warning period, on the outbreak of war, and, in case of any enemy penetration into a particular sector, during the course of the war itself. At all times, the practical and physical protection of the forward-most zone, which is generally described as the "border" or the "border area", will have to be catered for and in the most effective manner.[14] In a technologically rapidly-changing world, this is not an easy task. In this study, all the successive layers of defence, from the forward border zone backwards, cannot be discussed in detail. Some details will be necessary for the forward-most zone, and some of the necessary operational and organisational policy for the next layer will be necessary, because of its inter-relationship with the forward-most zone. Such a defensive battle scenario has been spelt out in this study, in order to put into perspective the measures under discussion.

*The Army's Multiple Roles*

In spite of its perceived and mandated "border defence" role, a reality today is that the army is actually simultaneously struggling to be four different armies in one. It finds itself juggling four differing, though overlapping, sets of responsibilities at the same time. Thus it is, concurrently: (1) a "border defence" army; (2) a counter-insurgency (COIN) army in certain frontier regions; (3) a conventional "strike" army prepared for mechanised warfare; and (4) a nuclear-armed army prepared to fight a tactical nuclear battle, if necessary. Each of these disparate responsibilities require special armament and equipment and the organisations to match. They also require differing operational level and tactical doctrines, and most important and difficult of all, different mindsets and attitudes, requiring different operating mind-sets at both the officer and the PBOR level. Though there is a certain amount of necessary arms and equipment overlap between (3) and (4) above, the operational level and tactical levels require drastically different doctrine and practices at the functional level on the ground.

Due to the structure and manpower organisation policies of the basic branches of the regular army, these various operational functions have to be carried out in rotation by the same functional units, i.e. the battalions of the infantry, or regiments of the artillery and combat engineers. For these combat or combat support arms of the army, permanent role-specialisation within a specific border sector, in any of the four major operational roles, is not a practical solution from the overall management point of view.[15] For some equipment-specific arms/branches and specialised units, to some extent only, is it practical to specialise for a particular role in a particular sector of the border. Examples are the tank regiments, the mechanised infantry battalions, and the bridging regiments of the engineers. For the more "generalist" arms such as the infantry, artillery and the generalised combat engineers, specific locational role capability will therefore automatically vary, depending upon the length of time spent in that specific border sector and the amount of preparation put in. Due to this inherent variability in the readiness of units available in any sector at any given time, the pros and cons of some fighting organisations that are role- and location-specific, need to be studied. An organisation such as the Territorial Army can more easily be given regional or terrain-specific roles, and the arms, equipment, and organisations to match, even though this is not the case at present.

Over and above the normal readiness requisites of unit rotations through various sectors, the army is saddled with the recurring necessity of providing "Aid to the Civil Authority" for a wide range of additional tasks. These range from "Internal Security (IS) duties" essentially for maintaining law and order, to disaster management in the event of natural calamities, and include "out of area contingencies" such as the tsunami in Sri Lanka, the earthquake in POK, and the cyclone in Bangladesh. These responsibilities detract from and reduce the location- and role-specific training and practice time available to the constituent units of fighting formations which have border-related operational roles.

In this complex situation, it becomes necessary to study the options and the roles of the army and of all other government organisations expected to function in conjunction with it. This would cover the methods possible for optimising national resources to discharge these different responsibilities, and the planning and organisation for likely future scenarios. This needs to be done separately for each of the Army's four major functional responsibilities mentioned above. Since this study is only looking at the border defence function, i.e. the safe-guarding of territory, the others are not being discussed, even though they may have to be undertaken in the border zone.

*Border Defence in Practice*

For practical reasons of efficiency, it is not possible to keep the Army fully mobilised and deployed for war. Nor is it cost-effective at the national level to physically protect the borders by using the Army on a full-time basis. The border, therefore, can best be manned permanently by a police or quasi-military organisation organised as a border para-military force,[16] which can be called Border Guarding Forces (BGFs). On its part, for a scenario of war, the Army has catered for a certain number of field formations[17] and their subordinate units, to be located in military stations and cantonments located as close as possible to the borders. These will be the first to react defensively by quickly occupying their pre-planned forward defensive positions. Larger numbers of formations, as needed under the existing planning, will be moved forward in a pre-planned manner once the mobilisation gets under way, to arrive and occupy their defensive positions within an acceptable time-frame. The field formations of the Army that are tasked with occupying such defensive positions are generally spoken of as "holding formations" or more commonly presently, as "pivot formations". Simultaneously, other formations that have an offensive tasking, known as "strike formations", would be moving to their pre-planned concentration areas. Contingency planning for all possible threat scenarios on the probable or likely threatened borders generally cater for both types of tasking.

*The Army's Border Defence Planning*

Existing broad Indian defensive planning apparently continues to function on the premise of a "one-and-a-half-war" scenario, with the main war to be fought with Pakistan and a simultaneous "half-war" or limited border war with China. This presumably is the "Two-Front War" contingency alluded to by Gen Deepak Kapoor, India's previous Chief of Army Staff, which caused so much consternation in Pakistan in 2009-10. Since both Pakistani and Chinese offensive strategies include attacks on rear areas, both in the border zone and far into India's hinterland, these offensive actions are no longer going to be confined to cross-border actions in J&K alone. Therefore, it is felt that, in the current threat scenario, the existing contingency planning may not be able to effectively take care of the enhanced threat from forces composed of so-called "non-state actors". The question, therefore, arises as to whether the present policies and practices being followed are the most effective way to deal with the current simultaneous threat to India's borders and India's rear areas from the border zone backwards.

War planning for the India-Pakistan border in the plains, has, since 1965, included plans for an Indian counter-offensive by the strike formations. It is generally accepted that such a counter-offensive would be, at the least, mounted by more than one division-sized armoured formation, under one or more offensively-tasked Corps HQ. But there has been one serious qualitative change in the last decade. As a result of the large-scale Indian practice military maneuvers code-named "Exercise BRASS TACKS-IV" and its immediate resultant "Operation TRIDENT" in the winter of 1986-87, Pakistan undertook weaponisation of its nuclear programme on an urgent basis.[11] The Indian (Pokhran-II) nuclear tests of 1998 and the follow-on 'tit-for-tat' tests by Pakistan immediately placed plans of "deep strike" into the plains of Pakistan under a nuclear cloud of uncertainty. This has led to an increase in Pakistani self-confidence and assertive aggressiveness in both its foreign policy and military strategy. The Kargil intrusions by Pakistan of 1998-99 and the Mumbai sea-borne suicide attack of 2008 by ostensibly non-state actors were a direct outcome of this combination of confidence and aggressiveness. This strategic development has led to an even greater political necessity of a water-tight border defence by the Army.

The broad planning for border defence, as applicable for India's threatened Pakistan and China borders, envisages a rapid general mobilisation, along with a simultaneous occupation by forward-located field formations of critical parts of the planned border defensive deployment. This general pattern remains applicable to borders in plains terrain as well as in the mountains. It includes the forward concentrated location of defensive reserve formations and units tasked for local counter-attack, meant to restore the situation where an enemy attack has actually penetrated the forward border defences and entered some distance into Indian territory. The defensive layout itself varies from sector to sector, as per the actual terrain and the likely enemy threat on the anticipated enemy route(s) of ingress.

### *The Defensive Battle*

Since the Army is not physically occupying most of the Indo-Pakistan or Sino-Indian borders, the occupation of forward defences by the Army involves co-ordination with the para-military BGFs which physically man most of the borders in peace-time. These BGFs are expected to withdraw from all but the least-threatened segments of each sector when the Army moves forward and occupies its border defensive posture. The development of a defensive battle against an ingressing enemy at the border would most likely follow the general pattern given hereafter:

- Threat of war develops.
- General mobilisation of India's armed forces ordered.
- Field formations of the Army in forward cantonments deploy to pre-planned border defensive positions.
- BGFs withdraw to rear areas for rear-area security tasks.
- Defensive reserve formations and offensively-tasked formations move to operational locations or concentration areas.
- Enemy attacks border at point(s) of its own choosing.

- Possible enemy penetration of one or more forward-most defensive positions.
- Local counter-penetration posture adopted by forward field formation affected.
- Local counter-attack launched by the available reserve of the holding formation.
- Holding formation adopts counter-penetration deployment posture where the situation permits.
- Counter-attack by sector/theatre reserve formation to destroy ingressed enemy forces or evict enemy ingress.

The above general description forms the basis for the discussion on border defence and peace-time border management for the rest of this study.

*Fighting a Border War with No Loss of Territory and the Requirement of a Reserve*

The political term of reference given to the Army for defending national integrity stipulates "no loss of territory". It, therefore, requires an adequate strength deployed forward along the borders at the shortest possible notice, to cause serious pause to an attacking force at the very border itself. This imposes enormous operational and tactical constraints upon the Army in its planning and preparedness for fighting an appreciated defensive battle. Since halting an attacking force at the border requires sufficient troops on the border and in the immediate forward zone, adopting a "trip-wire" type of forward deployment[18] is not an available option. The imposed pattern of forward defensive posture, therefore, becomes of the "hard crust" type, with a "thick crust" in critical or vulnerable areas, and a "thinner crust" everywhere else. Therefore, an overall resultant "thin crust" pattern of forward defences is now the norm for the IB with Pakistan in the southern-most part of J&K, the entire Punjab border, and in northern Rajasthan.

Such a binding stipulation at the national and Army Command level converts a political strategy into an operational policy for the defensive Corps Commanders concerned. Below their level, it becomes a tactical method of deployment along a DCB or other linear obstacle. Operational "art" consequently becomes a misnomer, and tactical ingenuity non-existent, in what becomes more or less a mathematical deployment of units and sub-units over pre-determined distances. The only flexibility possible at both tactical and operational level becomes the variability in the location of reserves, and the actual timing of their employment in a defensive battle. These reserves, designated or "created" from the infantry company level upwards, are meant therefore to be employed only for immediate counter-penetration, local counter-attack, and counter-attack at the division and Army Corps level. The deployment pattern and the wide lateral dispersal imposed means that a formation once deployed will be hard put to lift troops even for a small spoiling attack onto an enemy forming up for assault. This rigidity of the deployment method is what constitutes a major weakness of the linear "thin crust" defensive deployment. But it nevertheless suits the Indian requirement in the western plains sector facing Pakistan, in southernmost J&K, the Punjab, and in northern Rajasthan. In a modified form to adjust for the mountain terrain, the same philosophy has been applied along the LoC and AGPL in the rest of J&K, in order to prevent any loss of territory.

The serious problem with this kind of deployment is that for it to be effective, it has to deploy as great a number of units as can be mustered onto the forward obstacle line, to "thicken", i.e. strengthen, the line and thus the overall "crust", as much as possible. A practical reality is that at any point in time, the number of combat troops available all over the country in any operational situation will always be limited. There is a real need for adequate forces in reserve, either deployed to hold a vulnerable rear area, or held concentrated for quick movement to react to enemy moves. Locating the maximum number of combat units forward, and thus, more or less inextricable deployed on the borders, leaves not much available as a concentrated reserve at locations in depth. This dichotomy ensures that there will always be a shortage of troops for a more secure defence of the country's entire landmass.

Creating a larger Army with more combat units composed of long-service regular troops with life-time benefits is getting increasingly expensive, and so there will always be a financial or practical limit to expansion. In the two World Wars, linear defensive deployment was employed in many places by different countries, but for the major powers in those wars, manpower was not so much of a problem. The entire nation went to war in a national effort, and those wars were not fought by purely professional armies.[19] The major armies, navies and air forces of the world were composed of *all* the able-bodied men of the entire nation, under the legal obligations in each of those countries which obligated every able-bodied male citizen below a certain age to serve in the armed forces.[20] Practically the entire manpower of each country fought for the survival of their nations in their respective national armies. Such a luxury in the availability of manpower is not available to India, with its cost-limited professional army.

After examining the issue, the inescapable conclusion is that the preferable solution would be to have the largest possible number of fighting troops the country can manage, both on active service and in reserve. This would mean having entirely adequate numbers of fighting formations available to deploy on or near the borders to effectively implement the political directive of "no loss of territory acceptable", and at the same time, having a large enough available reserve for offsetting reverses in any sector, as also for a war that might go on for longer than anticipated. The presently available ground forces do not appear to be adequate for any geo-political scenario that adversely changes the present threat calculations. The availability of adequate numbers of well-trained and properly integrated reserve forces would make a great difference to India's border defence potential.

## Strategic Threat Assessment and its Budgetary Support

A cross-border surface threat of war from one of India's neighbours, or through the territory of a neighbouring country, constitutes a threat requiring a military defence of the country's borders. The likely threat of a hostile government's attack onto Indian soil across India's land or maritime borders is, in the present geo-political circumstances, restricted to possibilities only from Pakistan or China. India's borders with Bangladesh, Myanmar, Nepal and Bhutan do not appear threatened by cross-border military attack. The threats from China and from Pakistan therefore merit amplification, and are examined separately.

Since the 1962 Sino-Indian border war, defence matters have regained the attention of the political leadership. Nevertheless, it can be seen that defence planning since then has not always been entirely based on cold military logic in the broadest sense. Major Jaswant Singh,[21] has been India's Minister of External Affairs, the country's Finance Minister, and also briefly Defence Minister, and is thus experienced at the highest levels of Indian policy-making and implementation. He believes that there is a mismatch between the long-term cross-border threat to India, and the budgetary resources allocated for it. His view broadly is that the threat from China is greater than that from Pakistan, but budgetary allocations have been skewed towards the more immediate threat from Pakistan, without adequately catering for the greater one from China. Writing in 1999, he stated that "The 1962 winter war with China was a watershed.... The programmes that were realised make sense only if it is assumed that in the 15-year defence plan framework ending around, say, 1978, the chief concerns were to develop capabilities to deal with primarily landward threats from China and Pakistan."[22]

It is well-known that the post-1962 military growth in India was undertaken because of the twin China-Pakistan threat, and the subsequent force was planned on the basis of the capability to fight two wars at the same time. Jaswant Singh believes that "the substantive growth in operational strength was keyed to the demands of the western front." He argues for a realistic and proportionate correlation between the threat assessment and the budgetary support for it, as practically demonstrated by the allocation of expenditures towards the perceived threats. He believes that India had not been doing this correctly for many years. He elaborates the strategic China and Pakistan contexts as under:

> The China threat, meanwhile, remains unaddressed in its larger context. But it is narrowly conceived as an inaccessible border problem able to be adequately dealt with by the mountain forces in place, which at a maximum, are designed to prevent a repeat of the debacle in the 1962 war, and by political moves towards compromise and accommodation. An asymmetric military relationship with China is compensated by a military build-up against the manifestly lesser adversary, Pakistan. This then is the basic policy map apparently used by the MoD for force planning purposes and reflects an inflexible threat assessment, which has remained unchanged virtually since Independence, in a period encompassing major geopolitical upheavals.[23]

He elaborates the mismatch between the overall strategic threat and budgetary allocations to the armed forces thus:

> By 1964-65, nearly 82 percent of the authorised mountain warfare capability was already in place, with no further major expenditure undertaken in this field. No major weapons meant specifically for over-the-Himalayas kind of operations were acquired as an obvious follow-up.
>
> The disproportion in the budgetary support of mission capabilities becomes even more marked. The spending on armour and plains infantry, together accounting for just over half (50.45 percent) of the entire defence allocation in 1997, is 4.5 times that on mountain divisions, in excess of 49 times the total expenditure on the Navy, specifically, 120 times that on the sea control

> and coastal defence assets and nearly 297 times the sea denial capabilities afforded by submarines—the only effective means of deterring hostile activity off peninsular India which, defence-wise is the country's weakest, most vulnerable, frontier.
>
> There has to be some correlation between defence expenditures and the threats supposedly faced by the country. Such resolute and sustained weighting of defence expenditure on the side of certain select war-fighting capabilities at the expense of other capabilities to deal with equal, if not more serious, threats naturally raises doubts about the efficacy of MoD/Defence Services' so-called 'threat-based' requirements planning. Assuming that there is a correspondence between the threats and the defence expenditure, then, to justify the investment/ongoing expenditure in armoured and plains warfare capabilities, the threat from Pakistan would have to be some four times as great as the one posed by China across the mountains. But is that the case? And this Pakistani threat, moreover, would have to be nearly 50 times as onerous as the threat from any source on the sea. Again, is it so?[24]

The purpose of quoting from Jaswant Singh's treatise on the defence of India is not to point out weaknesses either in budgetary allocations or in threat analysis, but to highlight the very important need to allocate resources of money, men and material to border defence, based upon actual threat assessments. The physical threats to India's borders need to be prioritised as well as quantified in order to allocate the appropriate funding for the military task envisaged. Such geographic-sector prioritisation will further have to be divided into a temporal division between peace-time threat and war threat, since these are presently handled, in principle, by two different ministries of the Central Government. As border defence and border management are presently organised, allocations to cater for estimated war threats will be for the MoD, while for the peace-time threat, they will be divided between the MoD and the MHA.

Assuming that the necessary expenditures on threatened borders are necessarily to be more than on the less-threatened or non-threatened ones, the initial division of allocations should be between the war-threatened and the others. If it is assessed that the threat to India's territorial integrity from China and that from Pakistan is equal, it would be logical to assume that, over the long term, expenditure on tackling both the war threat and the peace-time threat on the borders with these countries should be on a 50:50 basis. This planned expenditure could then be divided between expenditure for meeting the war threat and for protecting the border in peace-time, based on existing shortcomings, planned improvements and so on. Other allotments could then be based on the peace-time border protection requirements of those borders not presently threatened by war.

Supposing that it is assessed that the existing territorial threat from Pakistan is greater than that from China, taking into account that the LoC-AGPL constitutes a "live" border, hypothetically, in a 60:40 ratio, then, over the long term, the financial allotments should be allocated in the same proportion. Within the allocation for the Pakistan border, it may be assessed that the threat of a major land offensive from across the IB has now lessened, after the establishment of a nuclear weapon parity. Therefore, it may be further assessed that the likelihood of a war threat for the capture of Indian territory exists more in J&K than in the plains, perhaps in the order of 70:30. In such a circumstance, financial allocations should be on that basis, after assessing the existing situation and existing shortcomings/desirable improvements where applicable.

## NOTES

1. See, for example, the discussion in Lorne J Kavic, *India's Quest for Security: Defence Policies, 1947-1965* (Berkeley, CA: University of California Press, 1967), p. 86. The border with East Pakistan, now Bangladesh, had not initially aroused such insecurity amongst residents in the Indian border zone.
2. This may or may not involve additional military defence policy options, such as an offensive defence policy that seeks to protect territorial integrity by launching offensive action across the country's borders.
3. Ministry of Defence, "National Security Environment: An Overview," http://mod.nic.in/aforces/welcome.html, accessed on 21 July 2009.
4. "National Security Environment: An Overview," www.mod.nic.in, as cited in Gurmeet Kanwal, *Indian Army Vision 2020* (New Delhi: Harper Collins, 2008), p. 91.
5. The length along the non-agreed and un-demarcated LAC has been given as 3,439 kms by Lt Gen Vijay Oberoi (Retd), in "Changing Battlefields," *Force*, August 2004, p. 50, whereas it is 3,488 kms as per "Origin of ITBP—The 'Himveers' and National Security," *Indo-Tibetan Border Police Force*, http://itbpolice.nic.in/mar.htm, accessed on 21 July 2009.
6. Ministry of Home Affairs, Government of India, *Annual Report, 2008-09*, p. 24, http://www.mha.nic.in/pdfs/AR(E)0809.pdf, accessed on 30 March 2009.
7. The better-known part of this policy was Lord Curzon's decision to create a British-controlled "buffer zone" between British India and Afghanistan, situated within Afghan territory. Thus came about the 1893 agreement, meant to be valid for 100 years, of a British India-Afghanistan boundary known as the Durand Line. This

resulted in the creation of a North-West Frontier Province (NWFP), located between the Punjab province, which was sought to be protected from the Afghans, and the Durand Line. This NWFP was inherited by Pakistan, and has only recently, in 2010, been renamed as "Khyber Pakhtunkhwa".

8. As during the Kargil operations of summer 1999. Indian ground troops were under orders not to cross the so-called "LoC" (at that point in time, a misnomer) which had already been crossed by Pakistani forces. The Indian Air Force was placed under a similar constraint. Ground troops were thus forced to launch difficult and costly frontal assaults to evict the intruders.
9. Harjeet Singh, "India's Strategic Culture: The Impact of Geography," *CLAWS Manekshaw Paper* No. 10, 2009, pp. 1-2.
10. Pravin Sawhney and Ghazala Wahab, "The Changed War: All defence, no offence," *Force*, Vol. 6, No. 12, August 2009, pp. 20-27.
11. Gurmeet Kanwal, *Indian Army Vision 2020* (New Delhi: Harper Collins, 2008), p. 56.
12. Ministry of Defence, n. 3.
13. Ministry of Defence, Government of India, *Annual Report, 1997-98*, Ch. 3, para 3.1, p. 16. Subsequent annual reports have used more or less the same wording, as can be seen on the Ministry of Defence website, www.mod.nic.in.
14. The distinction between 'effective' and 'efficient' is important here.
15. In the Indian Army, entire units (i.e. infantry battalions or artillery and engineer regiments) are rotated as a whole after a specific length of time, say two to three years. This is a consequence of the 'regimental system' of organisation, adapted from the British Army, which has stood the test of time and wars. The US Marine Corps follow a version of the same system. The US Army, by contrast, rotates individuals through units in different operational or non-operational sectors, even though entire units and formations may also get rotated through operational sectors such as Iraq or Afghanistan.
16. Till 1965, this function was routinely performed in many sectors by armed police organisations of the concerned border state, while different CPFs looked after or safe-guarded borders with Tibet and Myanmar. After 1965, the requirement of a specifically-tailored CPF for border-guarding duties was realised and the Border Security Force (BSF) was created, primarily for the Indo-Pakistan IB with West Pakistan.
17. Whether brigades, divisions, or Army corps.
18. This implies the tactical deployment of a relatively thin "line" of temporary forward defences along the border or in the border zone, tasked to delay ingressing enemy forces for a short period of time, while a strong mobile reserve force held concentrated further to the rear prepares to engage and destroy the enemy force within own territory.
19. The only volunteer professional army fighting in both World Wars was the Indian Army of the British Empire. In the Second World War, it was 2.5 million-strong, comprising men from undivided pre-Partition India.
20. Evading conscription was a punishable offence. Conscript soldiers, who composed

the bulk of the fighting forces, were not required to be paid "living wages" or given any pensionary benefits, as by serving, they were performing a national obligation.

21. He was an officer in the Army's Armoured Corps, belonging to the tank regiment "The Central India Horse".
22. Jaswant Singh, *Defending India* (Bangalore: Macmillan, 1999), p. 247.
23. Ibid., p. 250.
24. Ibid.

# CHAPTER 7

# A 'Second Line of Defence':
## Border-Guarding Forces and other Central Forces

### The "Second Line of Defence"

The armed forces of India comprise what is sometimes called "the first line of defence". Various other organisations have been created over the years since Independence, which are supposed to constitute a "second line of defence" as their primary or secondary role. Central forces of various kinds, which include the different BGFs and the Central Reserve Police Force (CRPF), as well as the military Territorial Army (TA), and the civilian student-based National Cadet Corps (NCC), are all supposed to be a "second line of defence", as per the reasons for their creation and the definition of their roles. In reality, in today's military scenario, none of these actually have the functional ability to be a true "second line of defence". On the ground, therefore, in the border zones of the Indo-Pakistan and Sino-Indian borders, there is only a "first line of defence", the Army (including the TA in the immediate "rear areas" of the border zone), and then, nothing else. In the air, it is the Indian Air Force and then nothing else, and to seaward, there is the Indian Navy, which is backed up to a very limited extent in inshore waters by the Coast Guard (CG).

Yet the issue of the "second line of defence" is of vital national importance. In India, the concept was given its due up to and through the 1965 and 1971 wars, but the euphoria following the 1971 victory led to national complacency. After the Indian and Pakistani nuclear explosions of 1998 and their consequent qualitative changes in the national security scenario, the issue has slipped from the national consciousness.

Not having a "second line of defence", in strictly military border defence terms, leads to either of two serious consequences:

- First, it imposes upon the country a requirement of having to create and maintain much larger, and thus more costly, regular armed forces than might otherwise be necessary. It forces the Army, in particular, to plan its border defensive operations keeping sufficient reserves of fighting field formations as a contingency back-up, in case the defensive planning does not work, and the defensive formations deployed are actually defeated by the enemy. This emergency back-up reserve would have to be over and above the field formations held concentrated elsewhere for a counter-offensive strike into enemy territory. If the plans succeed and the defensive and counter-strike operations progress well, the reserve will not need to be brought into action at all. In other words, they should never really need to be used, but will have to be created anyway and, it is hoped, never used. This is an expensive and thus inefficient manner of organisation. But possibly, an additional reserve cannot be created, for reasons of cost or otherwise. In this case, the border defence plans and their counter-strike component will either have to be made less ambitious, or will be less effective.
- Second, supposing the main defensive plans and the counter-strike plans all fail, and the enemy's armed forces gain initial victory, what is to prevent them from progressing their operations further? What will stop them, for example, either at Panipat, or on a beach near Vishakapatnam, or in some part of Arunachal Pradesh? Who will then oppose an assault landing by an enemy marine amphibious force, supported by ground attack fighter aircraft and naval gunfire, or an enemy ground advance spearheaded by tanks and fighter aircraft? Will India then be forced to capitulate? That this is not a purely hypothetical question can be judged from the fact that, in December 1986–January 1987, during the Indian 'Exercise BRASS TACKS-IV',[1] Pakistan's move of its reserve formations, to presumed offensive concentration areas opposite India's northern Punjab, resulted in a panic defensive deployment. This happened because that area did not have, at that time, any forces available for defensive tasks, with the army formations normally located there being involved at the time further south in the ongoing manoeuvres. If any second-line defensive

formations had been available to man the forward defences and to impose significant delay in case of a cross-border attack, there would have been enough time for the formations tasked and rehearsed for that area to move back from their exercise locations to the pre-determined locations of their normal operational tasks. Thus, a requirement for a "second line of defence" cannot be dismissed out of hand in the belief that such a requirement is illusory.

## The National Reserve Component

However, unlike India, most other major countries with large territories to protect, still continue take the issue very seriously. China and Russia both have reserve "second line" fighting formations in addition to their border-guarding formations of para-military BGFs, all of which are expected to fight proper military tactical defensive battles. Vietnam has a BGF organised into regiments (brigade-equivalent) and divisions. The Vietnamese border guards divisions, organised on the basis of local militias, fought China's PLA practically to a standstill when the PRC attacked Vietnam with 22 to 25 PLA divisions in March 1979. The Vietnamese regular army formations were deployed on the Cambodia front at the time, and were only involved later when some regular divisions were able to move back and re-deploy to protect the capital (Hanoi) and vital cities in the depth areas.[2]

Just to illustrate this thought process, it would be educative to see what level of reserves were being maintained by the US in 2005-06, which as in the case of India, are organised on all-volunteer basis:

- US Army: Active strength 502,000; reserve including Army National Guard: 676,150, i.e. over 100 percent of the active component.
- US Marine Corps (USMC), which includes infantry as well as all supporting ground elements such as tanks and artillery as well as an air component with attack helicopters and other ground-attack fighter aircraft: Active strength 175,350; reserve 92,000, i.e. over 50 percent of the active component.[3]

China's enormous PLA[4] has, in addition to its ground forces, an available reserve of 1.2 to 1.5 million-strong force of reserve and para-military units organised into 50 infantry, artillery and anti-aircraft artillery divisions. This warrants some amplification. The PLA is a military force composed of both active duty and reserve units, primarily responsible to defend China from external threats. The Chinese 2004 White Paper gives the total size of the PLA to be 2.3 million, of which the ground forces, i.e. the Chinese Army, is estimated to have about 1,600,000 personnel.[5] All reserve units have a backbone of active-duty military personnel, and are organised into platoons, companies, battalions, regiments, and above this level, into reserve brigades or divisions, but not above.[6] There is an additional 1.1 million-strong People's Armed Police (PAP) which provides internal security and border defence forces.[7] A third component of the armed forces is the militia. The PAP and militia are para-military organisations, and by law and definition, are not part of the PLA. Reserve units of the PLA carry out training in peace-time, and change to active units in wartime if mobilisation orders are issued by the government. Whereas the border defence forces are organised into regiments (Indian brigades) of three battalions each, the internal security forces are organised into regiments, divisions (including 14 mobile divisions) and corps. The secondary role of the PAP is external defence, and in times of war, the PAP's internal security units and higher formations can fight as light infantry supporting the PLA in local defensive missions. Generally, para-military forces are primarily responsible for law enforcement activities along the border, with the PLA in support. The PLA's border defence units are organised into regiments, and spread in company-size outposts along the length of the borders, occupying Observation Posts (OPs) and patrolling between outposts. Such PLA frontier defence forces units are lightly armed, and are tasked to provide early warning, but are not expected to fight a determined defence at the border.[8]

Pakistan has an Army of 620,000 active duty personnel and a reserve of 513,000. It also maintains large para-military forces totaling 288,000.[9] In the past, it has shown a propensity to use these para-military troops to either augment its regular troops as in Bangladesh (formerly East Pakistan) in 1971, or to use them for offensive low-level clandestine operations against India in the state of Jammu & Kashmir (J&K), or in conjunction with state-supported "non-state actors" and regular troops in Afghanistan up to 2001.

In the case of the US, which has "all-volunteer" armed forces since 1976, the National Guard and the Army Reserve, composed of part-time soldiers like India's TA, are two organised "second-line" military organisations, which are fully integrated into the operational plans of the regular US Army. The US thereby has a full-fledged "second line of defence" with its own units and formations, which are equipped at par with the regular army, complete with modern armour, artillery, and modern fighter aircraft such as the F-16. Part of the American "second line of defence", but distinct from the "Reserve", are the Army National Guard and the Air National Guard. These "second line" forces are organised into full-sized units under their own brigade HQ, and include armoured brigades, artillery brigades, and Air National Guard fighter wings.

Unlike the "first line force" of the US military, which is organised on a federal, i.e. central government basis, both the Army and the Air National Guards are organised on a "States" basis. Legally, they can be called out only by the respective Governors of states (the equivalent of India's Chief Ministers), and then placed under the command of the federal government. Individual units can be mobilised by their states, deployed on rotation for overseas operations and attached to regular US Army or US Air Force (USAF) formations. Entire National Guard formations can also be mobilised. The National Guard has fully organised and equipped infantry, artillery, and tank units, grouped into combat brigades of the National Guard, many of which are on the Order of Battle (ORBAT) of the US Army as "missing" or "round-out" brigades, tasked to join the designated divisions after mobilisation. After mobilisation, these are deployed on overseas missions as needed, to make up the complete ORBAT of their pre-assigned Army divisions. The Air National Guard has fully-equipped squadrons of modern combat fighter planes, capable of either homeland defence, or of deployment on foreign operational missions. Today, for example, there are National Guard units of various states of the US deployed in Iraq and Afghanistan and operating in the current operational tasks under regular formations of the US Army or the USAF.

The US Reserve forces, also based on part-time soldiers, but directly under the federal government, comprise the US Army Reserve, the US Navy Reserve, the USAF Reserve, the USMC Reserve, and the US Coast Guard Reserve. The US Army Reserve, unlike the Army National Guard,[10] provides additional logistical support brigades, which can be deployed overseas to further back up regular and National Guard formations. Like the National Guard, the Reserve is made up of volunteer, part-time soldiers, whose civilian jobs are protected by law if they are called up and deployed. They include many doctors, police officers and policemen, nursing staff, and other professionals who join Reserve-manned Field Hospitals, Military Police Battalions, and other logistics units.

Britain, which provided the basic organisational model for the Indian Army, though no longer a major military power, also has a "second line of defence" in the personnel and units of the Territorial Army Volunteer Reserve (TAVR). During the two World Wars, for example, Britain had its Territorials, upon whose basic recruitment philosophy India's TA was initially raised. This British TA of the time was organised into full battalions of infantry affiliated to regular regiments, fully-equipped tank regiments, and some artillery regiments. These Territorial units were sent to some operational areas and made part of regular formations, while others were grouped and organised into full field formations such as brigades and even divisions, and sent into battle when and where needed. In basic form, this system still exists as part of the British Army, the TA having got merged with the Reserve to become what is now known as the TAVR.

In India, with its different social system and attitudes, people with the necessary training and experience acquired during earlier Army service could perhaps be fitted easily into non-combat units appropriate to their military background. There was, in fact, in earlier years, a system of an Army "Reserve". When the system was last applicable, soldiers served in "Colour Service" for 10 years, and then remained on the "Reserve List" for the next five years. The ex-soldier with remaining "Reserve Liability" was recalled "to the Colours" in case of national mobilisation, reporting to a local Reporting Centre from where he was then sent back to his former parent unit in the case of combat soldiers. The combat unit could be far away at the other end of the country, but the soldier rejoined his former comrades, fitting easily back into his former company and often his old platoon, along with many of his former colleagues. The system worked well, provided there was plenty of warning to allow a slow mobilisation, as before the 1971 war. When the army actually went to war against Pakistan in November 1971, infantry units were at above their authorised strength levels because their Reservists had all rejoined. It was fairly simple for company-grade officers and Majors commanding companies to select some men from the available lot to be deliberately "Left Out of Battle" (LOB), without affecting the fighting strength and organisational composition. This old 10+5 years system[11] had to be later dispensed with for the sake of practicality, as the terms of engagement of the enlisted men (the *jawans*) had perforce to increase to the present 15+2, an almost universal basic 17 years.[12] In today's defensive philosophy, there is room for a modified Reserve system to function, to help thicken the "crust" by providing suitable manpower for logistical and other necessary military functions in the rear of the immediate tactical area. Any such system will have to build into it a purely localised employment of Reservists, to ensure a speedy tactical reaction. It will, however, require a great deal of consideration and some selective modifications to the existing organisation and war-fighting system.

It is possible and relatively simple to organise para-military forces into fighting organisations. Providing the requisite arms and equipment is also relatively simple: they can be stock-piled in advance and even procured relatively quickly. But it is neither easy nor quickly possible to give them the necessary training, the appropriate leadership, and critically, the necessary motivation. Most large countries with security requirements have grappled with this problem, and all have come up with their own answers. However, national security in a hostile environment does not come cheap, and the availability of forces to defend the borders requires a detailed examination. Therefore, we need to look at the existing organisations which could perhaps function as a "second line of defence". These are the Territorial Army (TA), the Special Frontier Force (SFF), the various BGFs [the BSF, the Assam Rifles, and the ITBP], the CRPF, and the NCC.

### *The Territorial Army*

The TA, an organisation composed of part-time soldiers and officers, with a certain amount of military training provided by the Army, was created soon after Independence, for the actual felt need and the very purpose of augmenting the Army's defensive capabilities at the borders. It is under the Ministry of Defence and both administratively and operationally controlled by the Army. The present role of the TA is to relieve the Regular Army from static duties and assist civil administration in dealing with natural calamities and maintenance of essential services in situations where life of the communities is affected or the security of the country is threatened, and to provide units for the Regular Army as and when required. Presently, the TA has a strength of approximately 40,000 persons, comprising of Departmental TA units such as Railway, IOC, ONGC, Telecommunication and General Hospital and other non-Departmental TA units. These are the Infantry Battalions (TA) and the Ecological Battalions (TA) affiliated to various Infantry Regiments.[13] Nuclear, Biological and Chemical (NBC) TA battalions are also being raised. Though the individual soldiers and many officers are part-timers, each unit is commanded by a regular Army officer and has a core of regular Army personnel. The units themselves are kept functional at all times and are never fully demobilised, even though they may not always be kept at full strength, owing to the part-time nature of the terms of engagement of the soldiers. The units of the non-technical TA units are basically lower-quality infantry units, and are affiliated with regular Army infantry regiments, which also provide the few regular Army officers. The TA is, therefore, smoothly incorporated into the Army's operational planning. It is used for guarding VAs and VPs in less-threatened areas, thus basically providing rear-area security in the threatened border zones. All units have personnel with ample military experience. They have been successfully used for both protective and patrolling duties even in COIN operational areas, such as the Kashmir Valley during the height of the separatist movement in the late 1980s and early 1990s. TA units were actively involved in military operations in 1962, 1965 and 1971.[14] The "Terriers", as they informally call themselves, have also taken part in "Operation Pawan" in Sri Lanka, "Operation Rakshak" in Punjab and J&K, and "Operation RHINO" and "Operation BAJRANG" in the North-East. The TA is an eminently suitable organisation for converting into a proper "second line" defensive fighting organisation for border defence. Its relevance and importance in the planning and organisation of Indian defence was highlighted soon after its inception by the late Lt Gen Th Nathu Singh,[15] who, along with Gen Cariappa and Gen Thimayya, was one of the "founding fathers" of the modern Indian Army of independent India. He had advocated a large complement of the TA, which would provide the "second line of defence", and would boost the resources of the regular army during war.

### *The Special Frontier Force*

The SFF is a military force operating under Army command for operational purposes, officered by Army officers, but with a semi-independent administrative set-up. It was created in 1962 with responsibility solely for the Indo-Tibetan border, though it has also been used in operations against Pakistan in 1971 and later in the high-altitude sector in J&K. PBOR are recruited from people of Indo-Tibetan background, who are ethno-genetically adapted to high-altitude living. It is intended for employment along India's high Himalayan Indo-Tibetan frontier. It is organised into battalions (also known as "Vikas" battalions)[16] which operate under the Army, and some independent smaller units which do not come under Army command or control. The SFF has a culture and operational ethos of its own, within a generalised military culture. The force overall is controlled at the national level by the Cabinet Secretariat. Being entirely officered by Army officers on deputation to the Cabinet Secretariat, the dualistic nature of its command structure at higher levels has not created either command or administrative problems.

*The Border Security Force*

Among the BGFs, the BSF can be taken as a basic example, as it was specifically created for the purpose of border safeguarding and of being a "second line of defence" where possible. As per its own official website, its role is: "Securing of border of India and matters concerned therewith." Its mandated tasks are:

During peace:

- Promote a sense of security among the people living in the border areas.
- Prevent trans-border crimes, unauthorised entry into or exit from the territory of India.
- Prevent smuggling and any other illegal activity.

During war:

- Holding ground in less threatened sectors.
- Protection of vital installations.
- Assistance in control of refugees.
- Anti-infiltration duties in specified areas.[17]

In the last few years, the BSF has, in addition to its border-related duties, been deployed for counter-insurgency (COIN) operations and internal security duties (IS Duties) as well.

The BSF was created for the specific purpose of safe-guarding India's borders in peace-time, with a clear understanding that they would be required to facilitate the taking over of the operational situation by the Army, where it was required to do so. It has grown over the years both in numbers and in capabilities, and now includes integral artillery fire support from its own Post Groups Artillery.[18] It was also clear from the time of its inception that there would be a necessity of BSF units being put under Army formations' command and control in some areas in peace-time, as well as in war. However, in spite of good and cordial inter-personal relations with the Army at all levels, areas of organisational friction have remained till date. This is primarily due to the controlling Ministries at the national level being different, exacerbated by the ingrained divisive tendency of Indians. In peace-time, both organisations follow two different systems of administration and logistics, including different and non-integrated accounting systems, with a resultant parallel logistics infrastructure. This duplication in operational areas is both a functional impediment and a national waste. Within BSF units, and at BSF formation HQ, such as a Sector HQ headed by a Deputy Inspector General (DIG), the prevailing "police culture", which is a different ethos from the "military culture" of the Army, occasionally causes hiccups in Army-BSF relationships. The other common cause for friction is the different promotion policies of the Army and the IPS-related promotions of BSF officers, which can result in Commandants of BSF battalions having less age and experience than corresponding-level Army officers. In spite of such petty inter-organisational differences, caused primarily by their being under two separate Central ministries, the two can work and fight together, though it is possible to find even better organisational solutions. The BSF, as constituted today, can be re-oriented into becoming a more effective "second line" of military defensive units than it is at present, with a very limited holding role. Its present role and equipment facilitates its tasking being enhanced slightly. This would be applicable whether the individual BSF unit is already under Army control in peace-time, or whether it is required to come under Army control on the declaration of military mobilisation, whether nationally or for a particular sector of the border. However, this brings into focus a more fundamental basic policy issue: whether a border police, organised as a CPMF under the MHA, should be organised to fight defensive battles supported by its own artillery even in "less-threatened sectors", a task that is the primary assigned task of the MoD. If indeed this is an organisational imperative, then logic dictates that such a BGF should at all times be an organ of the MoD, organised as a war-fighting BGF, designed to hold the border in sufficient strength and adequate capability to impose delay as a "trip-wire" force. Such a BSF would require to be fully integrated with the Army operationally and in ethos, to allow a smooth transition to the relevant Army formation's command and control once battle is joined, a tense and difficult period replete with the fog of war. To be battle-effective, such a BGF would have to be an MoD organisation, with a military ethos, which the present BSF is not. With a strength of 222,000 personnel, organised primarily into 159 battalions,[19] it is larger than the armies of many countries, and therefore, expensive. To be used to maximum effect for actual border defence when required, its apex control, chain of command in peace and war, and its cultural and operational ethos, all need to be rationalised.

*The Indo-Tibetan Border Police*

The ITBP is a CPF that is organised as a BGF, and is meant to come under operational control of the Army only in case of war. It has its own supply chain and arms/equipment stocking and maintenance facilities. It is officered by its own cadre of officers, and though battalions could be commanded by their own officers, it can and does have IPS officers at senior levels. It has its own advanced training facilities, even above the basic training stage. Officers of the force do not get trained or educated at the Army's advanced officer training establishments. No combined training, even at officer levels, is routinely carried out with the Army, either within the zone or in the theatre of operations. Inter-operability under enemy pressure is therefore suspect. The controlling ministry at the national level is the MHA.

*The Assam Rifles*

The Assam Rifles (AR) is a much older force, officered by Army officers on deputation to the MHA. It was raised by the British as far back as 1835, for maintaining British control over the entire north-eastern region, and is the oldest of India's CPMF. It has been through various name changes over the years, including Assam Frontier Police, and Eastern Bengal and Assam Military Police, till it acquired its present title in 1917. Its tasks have always included safe-guarding the external borders of the north-eastern region (in practice, the Indo-Tibet border in the eastern Himalayas and the entire Indo-Myanmar border), which is listed as one of its primary roles.[20] Internally, control was exercised through punitive operations. It remained at its original level of five battalions for many years up to 1947. Since the start of the Naga insurrection and subsequent insurgency from 1955-56 onwards, it was gradually expanded and also acquired a COIN orientation. Therefore, it is not typical of a BGF, because of the circumstances under which it was conceived and created. As a result of the various ethnic insurgencies in the entire north-eastern region, its organisation has been optimised over the years for COIN operations in this area. On the eastern Indo-Tibet border, entire units (battalions), or detached sub-units (companies), operate under Army control in forward areas, both in peace and war. It is now a large force of 46 battalions, and continues to be officered by Army officers on deputation. It has its own administrative and logistical organisations, which are used wherever the force operates on its own outside the Army's operational chain of command. Procedures have been worked out over time for the Army logistics chain to support forward elements placed under Army command, though only for limited support such as rations and medical cover. The controlling ministry at the national level is the MHA.

*The Sashastra Seema Bal (SSB)*

The SSB is a Central BGF which was converted to this role from an earlier role which included over-watch but not border-guarding. Functioning under the MHA, it now has the BGF role for the Indo-Nepal and Indo-Bhutan borders, on the lines of the BSF both in organisational structure and culture. Their BGF role is spelt out as being, "to prevent trans-border crimes and unauthorised entry into or exit from the territory of India." The SSB presently has 41 battalions and controlling sector HQ.[21]

*The Central Reserve Police Force*

The oldest and largest Central Police Force is the CRPF, originally titled the Crown Reserve Police before Independence. It had been created for augmenting local police forces for enforcing law and order. Prior to the creation of the BSF in December 1965, the CRPF actually had a border-guarding role, in addition to its primary role of being a reserve armed police force. At that time, the borders were mostly being protected by the armed police units of the border States. The CRPF's own website, on the Government of India's portal, lists "Fighting aggression during War time" as one among what it calls the "Broad gamut of duties performed by the CRPF."[22] It was while on border-guarding duties on 21 October 1959 that Deputy Superintendent of Police (Dy SP) Karam Singh and his 20 CRPF policemen were attacked by the Chinese Army at Hot Springs in the Aksai Chin border area of Ladakh. 10 policemen were killed and the rest were taken prisoners.[23] In the 1965 India-Pakistan war, two companies of the 2$^{nd}$ Battalion CRPF repulsed part of an infantry brigade of the Pakistan Army at Kanjar Kot in Gujarat. The CRPF has been designated the primary COIN force for internal security operations against left-wing extremism (Naxal terrorism), in addition to its other duties as an armed CPF for internal security and normal law and order duties. While it is a large and fairly well-organised force, re-orienting it to perform a combat role against aggressor foreign regular armed forces would be a difficult task. Due to its present organisational orientation, it is less capable of being converted to this role or being given such a task than the BSF. Nor would it be in the overall national interest to do so. It presently has 199 functional battalions, including 181 Executive Battalions, two Mahila (women police) Battalions, 10 Rapid Action Force (RAF) Battalions, six CoBRA Battalions optimised for a COIN role, plus one Special Action Group, and two Disaster Management (NDRF) Battalions, as well as Signals Battalions to provide communications support to their various HQ.[24]

*The National Cadet Corps*

During the 1965 and 1971 wars with Pakistan, NCC cadets were actually part of the "second line of defence" but in a non-combat role.[25] They organised camps to assist the ordnance factories, supplying arms and ammunition to the front, and were also used as patrol parties to capture air-dropped enemy paratroopers. NCC cadets also worked hand in hand with the Civil Defence authorities and actively took part in rescue work and traffic control. After the 1965 and 1971 Indo-Pak wars, the NCC syllabus was revised. Rather than just being the so-called "second line of defence", the NCC syllabus laid a greater stress on developing qualities of leadership and officer-like qualities. It was hoped then that many would be motivated to join the armed forces as officers. The military training which the NCC cadets received was reduced at the time, and greater importance was given to other areas like social service and youth-management. Today, the NCC has a greater emphasis on national integration than on any serious military capability.[26] The NCC as it exists presently cannot be converted into a "second line of defence" in any worthwhile military terms.[27]

Even a fairly short survey of the "second line of defence" and the BGFs as above shows that there are a number of overlapping jurisdictions, particularly in the case of the Sino-Indian border. In spite of the existing border defence system having evolved over the years since 1947 through the experience of external armed aggression, it can be seen that there are some shortcomings. An area of concern is the jumble of differing military and para-military units belonging to different forces that have been given operational defensive tasks in forward areas in the difficult mountain terrain along the Indo-Tibet border with the PRC. In some operational areas, all of the different types have been deployed, and those not initially under the Army come under command on the outbreak of hostilities. Many of these have their own separate administrative and logistical supply chains, all present and running in parallel. Differences in the quality of training and leadership exist. This situation is not conducive to fighting an effective defensive battle when the need arises. Some rationalisation would undoubtedly be beneficial, since duplication is both counter-productive as well as wasteful of the national effort. Some of the duplication appears to be the result of organisational "empire-building" with dubious justification for the border security effort.[28] The significant areas that need solution, improvement or streamlining are:

(1) Increasing the effective combat strength on the ground for a defensive posture against Pakistan in the agricultural plains.

(2) Improving and streamlining the defensive posture on the Sino-Indian border, by organising a more effective mechanism for better tactical tasking and for the transition to a war-fighting command and control system. Such an effort needs to address the aspects of national waste of effort where logistic systems are duplicated or even triplicated due to separate national-level ministerial allegiances for the various military and para-military organisations. There is a definite case for BGFs which are mainly going to be under Army command and control in war, and have some elements placed under the army even in peace-time, to come permanently under the MoD. In such a category may be considered the AR and the ITBP. While they merit transfer to the MoD, there is no concomitant operational requirement for them to be permanently under the command or control of the Army. The Regular Army, with its divisional and brigade HQ and subordinate combat and logistical support units and sub-units has well-practised border defence plans. Locally-employed Army units such as the various Border Scouts are already part of this organisational structure. Where the ground and deployment plan warrants it, they can function under the Army exactly as they are now tasked. The big difference will be that they will no longer come under the MHA, and whether under the army or functioning independently under their own controlling HQ in different sectors, they can become part of the same logistical and accounting system.

All army units of whatever kind in the operational zone come under the senior-most Army formation HQ, normally an Army Corps. The national controlling ministry for the entire border defence effort will be the MoD. This will both increase efficiency as well as reduce wastage of money and effort on the overall national scale.

## Peace-time Threats

An overview of the general nature of the non-military threats in peace-time provides a macro-understanding of India's border security problems. The Sino-Indian border, while peaceful on a routine basis, has the unresolved territorial issue and related boundary issue, and China's hardening diplomatic stance on this and other issues such as Kashmir has begin to worry India, to the point of augmenting its military readiness for the northern border.[29] The rapidly-deteriorating security situation in neighbouring Pakistan, and the rise of fundamentalism in Bangladesh, has aggravated the border security problems for India in both the east and the west. India's border with Nepal is an agreed political boundary, but one which cuts through a stretch of terrain that is identical on both sides, and inhabited by the same human communities. The Indo-Nepal border is politically an "open border", as citizens of both countries are legally allowed to cross into each others' countries. It is thus difficult to police, a requirement which has become necessary due to Pakistan's support to fundamentalist Islamic ideology in both India and Nepal, and its use of this soft and porous border for the infiltration of agents into India. The Myanmar border remains peaceful due to lack of any animosity or territorial dispute between the two countries, and also because the Naga separatist movement is now quiescent, following successive "peace treaties" with the Indian Government, even though the basic issue remains unresolved.

## Peace-time Border Management and the Army's Involvement

In theory, the Army should ideally have no peace-time border management responsibilities. In practice, this has not proved possible for India, starting from the 1947-49 Kashmir war with Pakistan. The friction with China, starting from 1959 and culminating in the 1962 war, left the Army manning the Sino-Indian border on a permanent basis in many places. In theory again, the peace-time border management policy, system, and practices, should all enable the smoothest and fastest possible transition from a peace-time control system to the planned war-fighting posture, both defensive and offensive. Failure to ensure this in the border areas could result in the same periodic surprises that hit India along the Sino-Indian border in 1962, in April 1965 in Kutch, and in August 1965 and May 1999 in J&K. The events of 1962 woke India from its slumber, to begin considering the necessary connect between diplomatic positions and military capability and training. 1965 brought about the creation of a border-guarding armed police force. The nasty shock in 1999 of the discovery of Pakistani intrusions in Kargil brought about the KRC. The KRC's and the consequent TF's recommendations were made on the basis of the situation obtaining in 1999. In some areas or in some aspects, the situation has undergone change in the past decade. More importantly, the KRC, the TF's, and the GOM's recommendations all pertain primarily to changes to be made for more effective peace-time functioning. None of them have actually reported on the planning and method of the war-fighting response, which could have, and should have been, far better.

It is the military defensive battle or offensive cross-border response that is the real protector of the borders, and is the acid test of the system. Therefore, the military defensive system is, by far, the most important part of overall national security. Its success or failure against intruding military forces is what determines the final result. Therefore, it is most important to devise a system that works, starting from the possible best war-fighting system, and going backwards to designing the best peace-time border guarding system. Any systemic changes that are recommended in the peace-time method should facilitate the quickest and easiest transition to the best war-fighting system. Otherwise, after the next episode of foreign military aggression on the borders anywhere, the system will be found wanting and yet another Review Committee will have to be set up.

The only problem with the "war-fighting first" approach is that the day-to-day peacetime functioning of border forces is a routine that is both difficult and tedious. It is also the norm for days on end, endlessly for months and years. A military threat or attack may not happen for decades. The human tendency will therefore automatically be to try and improve the peace-time functioning first. This will surely result in better peace-time border management, but may not best cater for or facilitate the primary requirement: to protect the border against foreign armed incursion. This study, therefore, looks at peace-time border management requirements, with the primacy of the Army's defensive war-fighting requirement always in mind.

## Peace-time Border Security and Border Policing

It was Pakistan's 9 April 1965 attack on one of the Gujarat Armed Police's Border Outposts (BOPs) in Kutch that triggered a fresh thought-process on the method of manning the borders in peace-time. The Indian Army Chief, Gen JN "Muchu" Chaudhuri, who had taken over immediately after the debacle of 1962, was instrumental in formulating the suggested new policy of creating a Central border police force. He was the first to suggest a well-trained police for peace-time border defence duties, with close support by the Army. This was accepted by the Central and concerned State Governments, and led to the creation of the BSF in December 1965. His own writings of the period are the best possible material available in open sources for explaining the rationale behind the new formulation. The rationale adopted at the time is the best guide for examining what should be the exact role of BGF today, based on the current requirements of transitioning from peace-time border security and routine border-guarding under no-threat or low-threat situations to an active military border defence.

Writing on 22 April 1965, soon after the Pakistani attack on Sardar Post, and just before Pakistan launched its 'Operation Desert Hawk' on 24 April:

> The recent happenings along the Kutch-Pakistan border and, in fact, continuous incidents along the Sino-Indo-Pak border as a whole, bring into prominence the whole question of how such a border should be looked after, in peace, in a cold war and when that war hots up. Should the responsibility lie with the police in the initial stages and if so, at what stage should the Army take over? What equipment should the border forces have, how should they be organised and under whose control should they act? How should liaison be maintained between the armed forces proper and a border force? Should the border be a State or a Central responsibility and how should the financial burden be shared? Police arrangements as constituted along the border at present seem confused and nobody seems quite sure, to quote from that otherwise unquotable limerick 'who does what and to whom'.[30]

"Muchu" Chaudhuri believed that the ultimate responsibility for the protection of the border, once war had been declared, should undoubtedly be that of the Army. The Army could be given a difficult section of the border to look after permanently in peace, as is the case along the LoC in Kashmir. Here, certain police forces would be placed under their direct command to assist them in their task. He warned of some of the inherent problems of border protection by stating:

> Incidentally, a big mistake in strategic thinking is to imagine that every inch of the border has to be guarded equally well. There are only small sections of the border, the violation of which means a sword thrust at the real security of the country. Violations elsewhere, such as the Kutch-Pakistan border, while irritating politically, are strategically only pinpricks of no major significance.

This suggestion had certain inherent problems. Gen Chaudhuri's deliberations on the subject examined four issues of importance, which are still of practical relevance today. He commented:

> Firstly, if a border police was over-sophisticated in organisation and equipment, it would certainly be too expensive for its general role. Secondly, with an over-equipped border police, there would be a very real danger of a border police post escalating a situation too quickly out of its own control. Thirdly, for close backing by the Army, who would decide, in terms of time, what is close? The mechanics and time involved in moving reinforcements even over reasonably short distances are time-consuming. Even after these military reinforcements arrived or were suitably positioned, time would be required to do the minimum essential reconnaissance before taking over. Further, in many cases, reinforcing the trouble spots might actually be bad tactics, it being always preferable not to reinforce failure but to hit elsewhere where the odds are better. If action by the police failed, then there would be the need for a quick transference of the problem to someone stronger, which would require close understanding between the police and the armed forces, with an effective system of switching control from one agency to another. Quick reinforcement would also require very close liaison. Finally, politically it would be better to guard a border with police because two police facing each other have less potential for real trouble than two armies facing each other. Attitudes are less rigid and talks simpler to begin, the very reason why mature countries prefer to have lightly-equipped border police forces manning their borders.[31]

On the subject of "Border Duties", he stated:

> An understanding of the factors that need to be taken into account for peace-time protection of India's borders is necessary. Border protection duties, under normal circumstances, deal with such matters as smuggling, dacoity, minor intrusions by civilians, both intentional and unintentional, the exacting of dues, the guarding of officials, the protection of installations such as railways or bridges and the establishment of counter-espionage measures. All these duties do not require very sophisticated arms, which are carried largely for self-protection, but do require a great deal of dispersion. Therefore, the armed police to whose lot these duties normally fall, work in small groups spread

over a wide area. These duties alone do not require a very high standard of military training or leadership.

Gen Chaudhuri felt that if these armed police were grouped together in battalions for tasks such as dealing with riotous mobs, hostile tribesmen, irregular forces or a brush with something stronger, their composition and training would need amendment, which has since been implemented. The issue of how much of the borders should be directly guarded at all times by the Army continues to be a practical issue today. Unlike an armed police, the Army, which keeps itself constantly trained to meet sophisticated and hostile armed forces, always works in a well-knit group, with each component fully integrated into the main plan. "Muchu" believed that splitting an army into small groups for a border police role would actually weaken the Army's potential and would be further weakened by not being able to use all its war-fighting equipment. Therefore, he felt, sending the Army out to look after every bit of the frontier would only do one of two things. It would either produce a huge, costly army of two parts, one designed for border protection, and the other for the normal, concentrated military role. Otherwise, it would result in a smaller army that had to remain dispersed to meet a border threat anywhere, thus becoming emasculated as an armed force which was ready to undertake its main and proper task.[32]

All the above arguments remain as relevant today as they were in 1965 when first articulated. The mission, capabilities, equipment, training, and command and control functions of the Border-Guarding Force (BGF) require some deliberation. This was gone into in July 1965. As decided, a BGF would be required to undertake normal police duties along a border including anti-smuggling patrols, the checking of illegal infiltration, anti-dacoity measures and the investigation of border crime. It would also be required to deal with minor armed intrusion until such time as it is relieved by the Army. Once it had been relieved by the Army for the responsibility of any segment of the border, it would be required to operate either under command or in conjunction with the Army, to continue patrolling quiet sectors and to guard certain vulnerable areas and vulnerable points. (Under the provisions of the 1949 India-Pakistan Cease-Fire Agreement, only armed police can operate within 500 yards of the Cease-Fire Line (CFL) in Jammu & Kashmir, and thus, these secondary military tasks were of particular importance for the security of the CFL.)[33]

The issue of arms for a BGF still needs debating. Whether it is the border police or the Army, eventually some group of individuals has to go and occupy the area of trouble or suspected trouble. Because of the different tasks and different threats to be faced, in the border police role, the requirement for very heavy covering fire should seldom exist. If a lot of heavy equipment is to be carried, mobility would be reduced and the number of men who could actually patrol and get on the spot would be correspondingly reduced. Therefore, for a border police battalion, the scale of equipment carried should be as light as possible, and yet, where required, a reserve of heavier equipment should be quickly available. What the Army calls 'Sector Stores' are one possible solution. Personal arms of the basic infantry types, along with Light Machine Guns (LMGs) at the scale of one per section of ten men should be adequate. The standard infantry 81 mm mortars and medium machine guns (MMGs) could be Sector Stores scaled as per the specific requirements of different sectors of any border.[34]

The urgency of the situation from April 1965 led to the decision to create the BSF. Its establishment took till 1 December 1965.[35]

Two important aspects of a border police force's functioning were commented upon by Gen Chaudhuri. The first aspect was liaison. Gen Chaudhuri's visualisation of liaison with the Army was a three-tiered structure. At Delhi, the headquarters of the Border Police Force (BPF) would maintain contacts with Army HQ. In the field, at each Command HQ, there would be a BPF liaison officer, while the DIGs responsible for sections of the border would maintain contact with the nearest major army formation HQ. Where a group of BPF units was working directly under the Army as, for instance, in Jammu and Kashmir, the controlling military HQ would have a DIG BPF as a functioning part of itself. The second was on geographical jurisdiction and command and control:

> In the border States where the force would operate, the command and control set up would require to cover a number of problems. Some of these would be the area of responsibility depth-wise, the legal position *vis-à-vis* the State concerned, liaison with the local police, the extent of authority to be exerted by the State Governments and, of course, the link-up with the nearest Army post.[36]

Against this initial rationale for a Central BGF, as put in writing in 1965 by the initiator of the present system, it is necessary to examine whether the border and territorial security situation along India's frontiers has changed qualitatively or quantitatively since then. In other words, have the requirements of border policing, as part of border security and border management, changed dramatically since 1965? In 2005, Dr GP Bhatnagar, a former Inspector General (IG) of the BSF, had characterised the situation on the borders, other than the Sino-Indian border, as under:

- Increased cross-border terrorism.
- Infiltration and exfiltration of armed militants.
- Emergence of non-state actors.
- Nexus between narcotics and arms smugglers.
- Illegal migration.
- Left-wing extremism.
- Separatist movements aided and abetted by external powers.
- Establishment of *madrasas* which could result in security hazards.[37]

Have the theoretical requirements of border policing, in both method and overall organisation, as spelt out in 1965, been adequately met? In this regard, Bhatnagar identified and listed the short-comings of the present system of border security:

- Deployment of multiple forces in the same area of operations.
- Lack of any doctrinal concepts.
- Organised as a series of knee-jerk reactions from a fire-fighting approach, rather than a fire-prevention or pro-active approach.
- Based on a strategy of "reaction and retaliation" rather than on a holistic response to a situation.
- Lack of co-ordination and synergy between the security management organisations.[38]

Gurmeet Kanwal, writing in 2008, has opined that: "Despite several border wars and conflicts, India's borders continue to be manned by a large number of military, para-military and police forces, each of which has its own ethos, and each of which reports to a different central ministry at New Delhi, with almost no real co-ordination in managing the borders." Identifying the issues for better border management, he suggested:

> While the BSF should be responsible for all settled borders, the responsibility for unsettled and disputed borders, such as the Line of Control (LoC) in J&K and the Line of Actual Control (LAC) on the Indo-Tibetan border, should be that of the Indian Army. The principle of 'single point control' must be

> followed if the borders are to be effectively managed. Divided responsibilities never result in effective control. Despite sharing the responsibility with several para-military and police forces, the army's commitment for border management amounts to six divisions along the LAC, the LoC and the AGPL in J&K and five divisions along the LAC and the Myanmar border in the eastern sector.[39]

To these must be added the two new mountain divisions for the north-eastern Sino-Indian border region, which were decided upon by the Indian government in June 2008.[40]

Kanwal had also commented in 2004 on the military's own command control arrangements, and on the overall Indian military commitment to the border in terms of permanent troop deployments. Citing an article in the print media, he observed: "Operationally, the Northern and Western Commands are responsible for military operations along the LAC, in portions of the Western Sector. The Middle Sector, on the Uttarakhand border, is under the operational jurisdiction of the Central Command, while the Eastern Sector along the Sikkim and Arunachal Pradesh borders comes under the operational control of Eastern Command." By contrast, he noted, "...on the Tibetan side, the entire LAC is managed by Border Guards divisions of the Chinese PLA under a single PLA commander of the Tibet Autonomous Region."[41]

Brig. Jaspal Singh, who has been a DIG of the BSF, has reviewed the current border policing arrangements and made a number of recommendations.[42] He opines that there is lack of direction and focus in India's border management, and that "mere increase in numbers will not suffice when one views the present arrangements of command and control, organisational structure, mission statements, and in that backdrop, the ability of these organisations to effectively absorb technology towards enhancing efficiency in their assigned missions."[43] His recommendations for BGF peace-time management re-structuring are as under:

- The entire Indo-Tibet border should be directly guarded by the Army and there is no requirement of any ITBP deployment.
- In J&K, the LoC and AGPL should be guarded by the Army. There is no requirement of BSF companies along the LoC interspersed among Army battalions.
- The ITBP and the SSB should be merged to form one BGF for the Indo-Nepal and Indo-Bhutan borders. India should renegotiate its

existing treaties to convert the existing "open border" to one wherein crossing would be permissible only at designated points.

- The BSF should be bifurcated into two BGFs, one retaining the name BSF, for the Indo-Pakistan IB, and the other for the Indo-Bangladesh IB, which, he suggests, could be called the Eastern Frontier Rifles (EFR).[44]

Further consideration of the actual requirements of these borders will show the extent to which his recommendations are valid. He also examined the practical aspects of the present organisational structure of the Central BGF battalions themselves, and their supporting units, and found that some changes are necessary. The main recommended changes are:

- All BGF battalions should be standardised on five functional companies only, instead of the six or seven that are presently prevalent, while the strength of each company should be increased from the present approximately 120 all ranks to 205 all ranks. He recommends that of these five companies, only three be deployed on the border at any one time, one held in reserve, and one be put through training in rotation.[45]
- BGF battalions should be authorised hand-held image intensifiers, Battlefield Surveillance Radars (BFSR), ground sensors and a much increased scale of modern communications equipment.
- BGF troops should be organised as lightly-armed scout forces, and the presently existing fire support units of mortars and artillery should be abolished. The money thus saved from the budget should be used for procuring the equipment recommended above.

It can be seen that some of the issues that were discussed in depth by Gen Chaudhuri in 1965 continue to remain inappropriately or ineffectively addressed even today. It is evident from the foregoing that, in spite of the situation on all the borders other than the Sino-Indian border having actually deteriorated, the issues originally identified have not yet been resolved in their entirety.

## NOTES

1. The two book length studies of the Brass Tacks crisis are (a) Ravi Rikhye, *The War that Never Was: The Story of India's Strategic Failures* (Delhi: Chanakya Publishers, 1988); and (b) Kanti P Bajpai, PR Chari, Pervais Iqbal Cheema, Stephen P Cohen, and Sumit Ganguly, *Brasstacks and Beyond: Perception and Management of Crisis in*

*South Asia* (New Delhi: Manohar, 1995). It is also covered in PN Hoon, *Unmasking Secrets of Turbulence: Midnight Freedom to a Nuclear Dawn* (New Delhi: Manas Publications, 2000); and in PR Chari, Pervais Iqbal Cheema, and Stephen P Cohen, *Four Crises and a Peace Process: American Engagement in South Asia* (New Delhi: Harper Collins, 2007).

2. Both sides claimed victory, though the Chinese PLA managed to advance about 25 kms along a wide front and took the city of Lang Son. Only one regular Vietnamese regiment (brigade) was employed in the war; deployed to join the border guards for the defence of Lang Son. On 06 March 1979, the Chinese announced victory in their 'punitive attack' and began to withdraw.
3. Gurmeet Kanwal, *Indian Army Vision 2020* (New Delhi: Harper Collins, 2008), p. 128.
4. This includes the ground force, the air force, the navy, the strategic missile forces, and reserve units for each component.
5. As per the International Institute of Strategic Studies, cited in Dennis Blasko, *The Chinese Army Today* (London: Routledge, 2006), p. 20.
6. Ibid., p. 22.
7. Kanwal, n. 3, p. 136.
8. Blasko, n. 5, p. 71.
9. Kanwal, n. 3, p. 139.
10. The National Guard has only ground or air combat units. When deployed with the Army or Air Force as an integral part of US field forces, the full-time regular forces incorporate them into their logistics and maintenance planning and support.
11. Itself a modification of an earlier 7 + 8 years system, in which soldiers were enlisted at the age of 18 years and then were pensioned off, unless promoted to NCO, at the age of 25 years, thus totally in agreement with the Indian sub-continental term "*jawan*" literally meaning "young" (man), and universally used to describe soldiers. This was changed to an 8 + 7 years system, and then to the 10 + 5 years system.
12. Further service is promotion-based. The system was designed both as a welfare measure to ensure a certain minimum length of career, and as an inducement for recruitment.
13. Indian Army, "Territorial Army," http://indianarmy.nic.in/Site/FormTemplete/frmTemp1PLT3C.aspx?MnId=r33D6bLT6Nc=&ParentID=PN872GmDUDM=&flag=p, accessed on 30 September 2010.
14. The TA initially had various types of units such as Armoured Regiment (TA), Infantry Battalion (TA), Air Defence Artillery (TA), Medium Artillery Regiment (TA), Engineers Field Park Coy (TA), Signal Regiment (TA), EME Workshop (TA), Coast Battery (TA), ASC General Transport Company (TA), ASC Composite Supply Platoon (TA), and AMC Field Ambulance (TA). By 1972, these units had either been disbanded or converted to Regular Army, except the Infantry Battalions (TA).
15. In a formal appreciation written by him in January 1948 as a Maj Gen, and GOC UP Area, entitled "An Appreciation on the Defence of India" and sent to Army HQ. Its salient points are given in his biography, which is part of the book by Vinay K Singh, *Leadership in the Indian Army – Biographies of Twelve Soldiers* (New Delhi, Sage Publications, 2005), p. 77.

16. Gurmeet Kanwal, "Indian Border Security: Poor Management in Evidence," *IPCS Issue Brief,* No. 55, October 2007, http://www.ipcs.org/pdf_file/issue/380296651 IPCS-IssueBrief-No55-GurmeetKanwal.pdf, accessed on 01 November 2007.
17. Border Security Force, Ministry of Home Affairs, "History & Role," http://bsf.nic.in/introduction.htm, accessed on 03 July 2009.
18. Possibly organised into seven BSF artillery regiments. See Mohammaad Zainal Abedin, "Fake Stories of Bangladeshis Intruding Into India," *Global Politician*, 08 June 2005, http://www.globalpolitician.com/2845-bangladesh-india, accessed on 21 December 2009.
19. Border Security Force, Ministry of Home Affairs, http://bsf.nic.in, accessed on 21 December 2009.
20. "Role and Tasks," *Assam Rifles – Friends of the Hill People*, www.assamrifles.com and www.assamrifles.gov.in, accessed on 23 September 2010.
21. Sashastra Seema Bal, www.ssb.nic.in, accessed on 23 September 2010.
22. Central Reserve Police Force, http://crpf.nic.in/crp_b.htm, accessed on 03 July 2009.
23. 21st October is now a day of homage, observed as Police Commemoration Day for the police all across the country.
24. Central Reserve Police Force, n. 22.
25. This author, a college student during the 1965 Indo-Pakistan war, was a member of No. 1 Gujarat Air Squadron (Flying) of the NCC's Air Wing. He was put on OP duties organised by the Indian Air Force on an outer ring around the city of Baroda, to report any night-time enemy air activity or parachute drops.
26. National Cadet Corps, www.nccindia.nic.in, accessed on 03 July 2009.
27. It does, however, have the scope of being converted into an auxiliary support to the regular forces in other ways, with imaginative and forward-looking policy changes. These would need to completely transform its present syllabus and system of functioning. A war-time role would also need either amendments to the present Act, or a completely new Act.
28. Kanwal, n. 3, p. 139.
29. See Arun Joshi, "More troops for Arunachal border," *Hindustan Times*, 12 November 2009.
30. JN Chaudhuri, *Arms, Aims and Aspects* (Bombay: Manaktalas, 1966), pp. 263-4.
31. Ibid., pp. 265-6
32. Ibid., pp. 264-5. This was written for precisely this reason, before the creation of the BSF.
33. As per the terms of the 1949 Karachi Cease-Fire Agreement, violated by Pakistan very soon after this was written.
34. Chaudhuri, n. 30, pp. 271-2.
35. It was started by incorporating existing armed police battalions of the Rajasthan Armed Constabulary (RAC) and the Punjab Armed Police (PAP), which had hitherto been responsible for manning the IB.
36. Chaudhuri, n. 30, p. 273.
37. GP Bhatnagar, "Border Security," *SP's Land Forces,* Vol. 2, No. 6, 2005.
38. Ibid.

39. "Seal of Trouble," *Force,* Vol. 1, No. 12, August 2004, cited in Kanwal, n. 16.
40. "India to raise two new mountain divisions of the army," *Express India*, 13 June 2008, http://www.expressindia.com/latest-news/India-to-raise-two-new-mountain-divisions-of-the-army/322331/, accessed on 21 July 2009.
41. Gurmeet Kanwal, "India's Borders," *Indian Defence Review*, Vol. 23, No. 1, October 2008.
42. Jaspal Singh, "Security of India's International Borders," *CLAWS Journal*, Winter 2009, pp. 118-30.
43. Ibid., p. 119.
44. An EFR actually existed prior to Partition and Independence, the two bifurcated components of which became what are now Bangladesh's Bangladesh Rifles (BDR), and an armed police force of the West Bengal Government still known as the EFR.
45. Singh, n. 42, pp. 129-30

CHAPTER 8

# Conclusion

The present system of border defence and border management has many strengths but some weaknesses as well. It is restricted by the national foreign policy not allowing a more effective military policy for defending the borders. Though India's defence policy is decided by consensus at the level of the Cabinet Committee on Security, the highest civil political body, it must be noted that Indian public opinion is turning in favour of a more retaliatory military posture for trans-border terrorism. This view is also therefore being expressed in Parliament, where Pakistan-sponsored or Pakistan-condoned terrorism is concerned. The extensive public and media debate after the terrorist strike on Parliament in December 2001, and that following the terrorist attack on Mumbai on 26 November 2008, indicates that the public mood in India is not to "turn the other cheek".[1]

The Parliamentary Standing Committee on Defence, in its 22nd Report, presented to Parliament in July 2007, had observed:

> National Security is a function of a country's external environment and the internal situation, as well as their interplay with each other. The traditional concept of national security has undergone fundamental changes over the years. It is no longer synonymous with sufficient military strength to defend the nation and its interests. Both the external and internal environment are changing at an incredibly fast pace, with developments in nuclear weapons and missiles, increasing cross-border terrorism, the emergence of non-state actors, the growth of Islamic fundamentalism, the narcotics-arms nexus, illegal migration and left-wing extremism, gravely impacting upon the security of the country. The rapid technological developments underway at the same time not only facilitate these events by reducing our reaction time, but add entirely new dimensions of threats and challenges.[2]

The defence of national territory is the primary function of the armed forces, with defence of the land borders being mainly the responsibility of the Army, assisted by the Air Force and by the para-military forces. Defending the borders to maintain the territorial integrity of the country is a war-fighting responsibility, but one which requires careful and constantly updated planning and preparation, including an appropriate defence policy. National security and defence policy-making and planning takes time. It has to consider the enhanced challenges and to come up with appropriate responses in terms of re-alignments of policy, re-organisation and augmentation or force increment as needed. Periodic review of existing policies and practices is therefore required. The last major review was that by the Kargil Review Committee of 1999.

This study reviews the border defence policy as well as the existing practices after a decade since the 1999 review, and recommends some modifications to be made well before the next border security crisis hits India. The suggested solutions for the new realities include suggestions for border defence and border management which can be applied without substantive changes to the present regime. In the realm of border defence, a major role for a completely re-organised Territorial Army (TA) with a new philosophy and a new operational role is suggested, to augment existing operational planning. It could usefully include a Reserve component, which needs to be created.

As has been seen, there are both macro-issues such as broad defence policy, i.e. offensive or defensive, and numerous micro-issues, such as the detailed functional policy for BGFs and their actual method of functioning, which are involved in optimising India's border defence and border management system. The issues of the best control, command and cooperation systems are contentious because they are subject to turf wars between central government ministries and their functional arms. In spite of the complexity and number of such issues, some broad truisms can be derived from the examination so far.

One is that a purely defensive territorial protective system is open to exploitation of the "Stability-Instability Paradox" by inimical forces across the borders, both in peace and war. This can perhaps only be mitigated by an avowedly retaliatory policy, used in carefully calibrated fashion. The other is that a purely defensive military tactical battle to be fought within own territory imposes upon the defender a requirement of quickly available large military reserves, pre-organised into what may be termed "second-line" formations such as "reserve infantry divisions", "reserve artillery brigades", and suchlike. This is so because without the availability of ample reserves, any border war that begins to go badly for the defender, will inevitably tend towards his fighting towards a cease-fire, instead of fighting for a win. In the worst-case scenario, it will mean a capitulation by the defender, as happened to Pakistan in the eastern theatre in December 1971. A cease-fire achieved under losing circumstances will result in a Cease-Fire Agreement that will be unfavourable and unsatisfactory. On the other hand, a cease-fire that results during a continuing fight-back, out of international pressure or due to cease-fire feelers from the attacker, will enable a favourable terminal agreement. Ample reserves, preferably vast reserves, are a national operational necessity for a country with a defensive policy, large borders to defend, and aggressively hostile neighbours.

A third truism is that the security problems of the state of J&K, which are both of a territorial protection nature as well necessitate as a combination of COIN and internal security, need a military response in addition to that of the civil administration. The potential for a similar simultaneous combination exists also in parts of the north-eastern region, and thus in a sense, the two are analogous. In J&K, part of the military response has been the creation and employment of the RR, which is fully under the MoD. In the north-east, the AR is organised and capable of fulfilling the dual functions of a BGF and a COIN force, one which is officered by the Army and even operates under the Army's command, but whose apex control is exercised by the MHA. This needs closer examination.

Some of the micro and macro issues which have general applicability and have been touched upon, but not examined in much detail, are looked at hereafter.

A number of the practical problems of border management in peace-time, which includes the actual policing function, emanate from differing legal positions in different areas, and the complexities arising from the applicability of different laws for related crimes to the same person(s). Other problems arise from the socio-economic conditions peculiar to particular areas of the same region and sometimes from the internal administrative problems of the BGF themselves. The basics of some of the issues, as a representative sample, are discussed in the succeeding paragraphs.

*Legal problems related to illegal immigrants:* This has been the most difficult problem along the Bangladesh border and in the north-eastern States where Bangladeshi immigrants have settled, always for better economic opportunities. It has been aggravated from the time when the Central Government managed to get an Act passed by Parliament that set aside the provisions of the Citizenship Act of 1955. The Illegal Migrants (Determination by Tribunals) Act 1983 (IMDT Act), changed the cut-off year in respect for Assam, for determining legal residency status in India, from 1951 as for the rest of India, to 1971. The Act appeared to be motivated by vote-bank politics. It legalised at one stroke the erstwhile illegal immigrants who had arrived between 1951 and March 1971, when the Pakistani crackdown on Bengalis in the erstwhile East Pakistan (now Bangladesh) began. It also made it well-nigh impossible to prove the illegality of the person's residence in India. Its results were a total flare-up of violence in Assam and the birth of the ULFA. Under the provisions of this Act, both the BSF and the State's civil police found it difficult to ever prove the illegality of border crossers, and became lax in actively pursuing the task of apprehending them. After much violence and atrocities committed on innocents, the law was contested in the Supreme Court, and eventually repealed in 2006. But the years in between saw many more Bengali Muslims from Bangladesh illegally crossing over and settling down, changing the demographic profile of Assam, thereby provoking political unrest and law and order problems, and creating an unstable internal security situation.

*Legal/administrative problems of jurisdiction of BGFs:* The civil administration and political establishment in some States or parts of States are sometimes not keen to allow the BGFs much physical space to exercise their legal rights with respect to border policing. This is particularly so in Muslim-majority areas in India along the Bangladesh border, where the locals have an affinity with the people immediately across the border.[3] Thus there are areas where the Indian local authorities and residents try to obstruct protective measures such as border fencing. Different States have ordered different distances into the interior for the policing to be the legal responsibility of the BGFs. This can be as little as four kms in some States, five in some others and 10 kms in yet others. These do not need to be rationalised because of the differing terrain and social conditions, but the BGFs need to be given the maximum cooperation by the State authorities in carrying out a national task.

*Economic and household necessities of the locals:* In the backward, poor and undeveloped border areas, again particularly along the Bangladesh border, accessibility to markets is often poor on both sides. There are many places where it is easier for the locals on either side to go to the nearest market, which may be across the border. Arresting such people merely turns the local people against the BGFs. It would be best to quickly conclude treaties with the Bangladesh government for legal trans-border trade in household goods and access to markets on either side, with some basic documentation. This is now in the process of being finalised with Bangladesh as a provision for "border *haats*". Such a local cross-border trade agreement has been made with China, even though its scope in items and in the number of such points are not at all adequate. Where control is needed is on the diversion of cheap Public Distribution System items, meant for the Indian rural poor, to traders across the border. The other measure that could be taken is to vigorously implement the Border Area Development Programme. Local revenue and development officials need to publicise the facilities offered under this scheme, and assist the border residents to avail of them, wherever feasible. The BGFs could be requested to associate to some extent with this effort, which would improve their standing with the locals.

*Lack of a proper identification system for Indian nationals:* This problem pertains to both illegal immigration and to border zone relaxations for residents of border villages. It is as applicable along the Rajasthan and Gujarat borders with Pakistan as it is for the Bangladesh and Nepal borders. The MHA had worked out a scheme in the 1980s for identification cards for the border areas. It had then been decided that these would be prepared and issued as part of a national scheme, the start being made from the border districts. The new Unique Identification Card scheme which is soon to begin should again start with the border districts. It does not expect to provide proof of citizenship, but merely of residence status, and could help resolve part of the problem of Bangladeshi economic immigrants if they could be given "foreign worker" status and placed on record.

*Differing stipulations for bailable and non-bailable trans-border offences:* Arrested smuggling offenders, if handed over by the BGFs to the Customs, are let off because the items may not warrant detention of the individual under the Customs Act, 1962. Some of these kinds of problems can be rationalised by legislating some over-arching legislation that allows the system to hold such foreign offenders till they can be tried for another simultaneous offence.

*Administrative and financial problems of holding detainees:* BGFs often do not have holding facilities for arrested illegal border crossers, particularly if large groups are apprehended. At the same time, the BGF battalions do not have any sanctioned funds for feeding such people. The authorities concerned would be well advised to attend to such administrative issues, which affect the actual functioning and enthusiasm for work of the BGFs.

## Bifurcation of Border Zone Responsibilities between Ministries

The greatly increasing internal security threat in India, from left-wing extremism as well as from Islamic fundamentalism, both internal and externally organised, requires a great deal more attention from the MHA. While it needs to retain the responsibilities for peace-time border security on some of the borders, it is suggested that it shed responsibility for security of the J&K and Sino-Indian borders. This responsibility should be transferred to the MoD, which is more responsible for these borders, at present anyway, having some BGFs of the MHA operating under Army control even in peace-time. This will reduce some of the MHA's workload, whose efforts can be devoted more towards dealing with the internal security threat.

It is suggested that MHA devote more attention to the cross-border illegal Bangladeshi Muslim immigration and the internal security problems that arise from it, and to the increasing influence of *jihadi* fundamentalists among the Bengali Muslims of India's North-east. In this connection, the activities of agents of the Pakistani ISI need to be carefully monitored and their networks penetrated.

Even for those border areas for which the peace-time security responsibility is recommended to be transferred to the MoD, the MHA should continue to retain the management of the Border Area Development Programme (BADP). The entire range of procedures that will facilitate the issue of identity cards to residents of border districts need to be addressed on priority by the MHA and the State governments concerned.

For the security of the borders which are already fully or partly under the Army in peace-time, the ideal solution is to have BGFs which are organisationally under the MoD. These borders are the LoC-AGPL in J&K, and the LAC along the Sino-Indian border. The most practical solution would be to allot the security of the entire J&K border, both the IB and the LoC-AGPL, plus the LAC with China, to the MoD. This would, in one stroke, eliminate practically all of the inter-departmental wrangles and turf wars, while allowing a common logistics infrastructure in the border area. The same principle should apply to the rest of the Sino-Indian border and the Indo-Myanmar border, where the AR are the designated BGF. In other words, the ITBP and the AR will both need to come fully under the MoD.

In the interim, the ITBP should continue to be responsible for the peace-time border in Ladakh (J&K), Himachal Pradesh, and Uttarakhand, as at present. However, they should be withdrawn from Arunachal Pradesh and Sikkim, where the AR are already present. In the eastern theatre, the AR and the Army together should provide the BGFs, while the Army continues to remain the Rapid Reaction Force.[4] The AR would thus combine the COIN and second-tier IS Duties responsibility for the northeastern states, along with being the BGF for the same region.

This suggestion, if implemented, will also mean the withdrawal of the BSF from J&K. The suggested re-allocation of responsibilities for border security between the MoD and the MHA will result in the MoD having to provide its own BGFs for some parts of the Indo-Pakistan frontier in J&K. One stretch will be the 198 kms of IB from the J&K-Punjab junction to the start of the LoC, and for the other sectors where BSF units are presently deployed on the LoC under Army control. If the Army does not want to secure these less-threatened segments by deploying infantry battalions, which are better used elsewhere or in other roles, the options for the MoD are to either raise the requisite number of battalions of a small para-military BGF, or create a small military BGF. This should not pose a problem, but would in fact, ease and improve matters. Such a force can be raised and manned without the seemingly insoluble problem of the lateral transfer of soldiers to CPF under the MHA, as has been recommended by various committees and even by the 6$^{th}$ Central Pay Commission. Such a MoD BGF would face no problems of inter-ministerial transfer, and the terms of engagement, salary structure, etc, could be worked out within the MoD itself. Middle-level officers of the Army could serve tenures in the force, each of whose battalions should have a Commanding Officer (CO), a Second in Command (2IC), an Adjutant, and a Quarter-Master (QM) from the Army. Company Commanders of the rank of Major could be from promotees from enlisted ranks within the force, in a manner similar to the Regimental Commissions being granted to Army JCOs. This will also provide an incentive for career advancement within the PBOR.

For such a MoD BGF, the other issue that will need to be addressed will be the question of the class composition of the entire force or of individual battalions. The choice is one out of two options: a "national army" type of class composition consisting of "All Indian Classes", or an infantry regimental-type with either a "fixed class composition" or "single class". From the Army's initial experience with the RR, it is recommended that the individual battalions be affiliated to existing infantry regiments, and accordingly have either a "fixed-class" composition, or be a "single-class" unit, as per the parent regiment. The manpower should also, therefore, be drawn from the respective infantry regiments. A military BGF, if this option is chosen, could conveniently be called the Rashtriya Rifles (Borders), or something similar. Administrative overheads would not significantly increase if the men are transferred from the affiliated infantry regiment after a specific number of years of service in their parent battalions. It would mean, at most, an increase of a clerk or two in the regiments' Records Office, and the increase of an accountant or two in the supporting Pay and Accounts Office (Other Ranks) [PAO (OR)]. This would not adversely skew the existing teeth-to-tail ratio. No additional Records Office would need to be raised and no additional Individual Running Ledger Accounts (IRLAs) for the men would need to be created. In case such a "BGF-type" responsibility for the Army is considered far-fetched, the existence of various Border Scouts may be cited as precedence. As another precedent, the Mahar Regiment presently has three battalions titled 4th Mahar (Borders), 5th Mahar (Borders), and 6th Mahar (Borders), which started in 1948 as the 1st, 2nd, and 3rd Border Scouts, before being merged into the Mahar Regiment and converted to normal infantry battalions. As yet another example, prior to the creation of the RR, a "31" series of infantry battalions had been raised in various infantry regiments, optimised for a COIN role. These were later converted to normal infantry battalion organisation and renumbered serially with the other battalions of the regiment. The concept, therefore, is not new.

## Border Management and Internal Security in the North-East

The Indo-Bangladesh border management problem is intimately linked to internal security in the north-eastern states, as has been brought out. In Assam at present, 40 percent of the State Legislative Assembly seats are being determined by the sheer numbers of illegal Bangladeshi immigrants.[5] Control of the border, and monitoring of the reported increase in Islamic fundamentalism among a basically survival-minded and economic-betterment oriented immigrant population are both MHA subjects, the first through the BSF and the second through the Intelligence Bureau.

Another related area of importance to which the MHA needs to devote its attention is the legislation relating to citizenship, illegal immigration of foreigners, and associated issues. The body of legislation is vast, and there are too many different Acts that are simultaneously applicable in many cases. A new and comprehensive Act governing the subject needs to be introduced, superseding all the previous ones. The problem of granting or not granting citizenship to the illegal Bangladeshi immigrants needs serious attention, and a compromise solution found, while all practical steps to prevent more immigration need to be simultaneously taken.

An important issue which the MHA needs to acknowledge, and act upon with tact and understanding, is that Assam and the other north-eastern States are different from the rest of India. Even though the Assamese and the Meitei Manipuris are Hindus, they themselves are not culturally part of mainland or mainstream India. The other ethnic hill-communities are even more different, mostly being speakers of different Tibeto-Burman languages, and have affinities with other similar and related communities in South-east Asia. The entire area had never been part of any Indian empire till the British Indian Empire, after defeating the Burmese in the First Anglo-Burmese War, annexed the Burmese provinces of Assam, Arakan, and Tenesserim from the Burmese kings in 1824-26.[6] Assam, Jaintia, Cachar and Manipur practically became British protectorates during this period, as the Burmese were debarred from interference in these areas. During the colonial period, the British Government viewed the region as a buffer between India and South-east Asia. They had, therefore, promulgated the East Bengal Frontier Regulations of 1873 to formally separate the administration of the region from the rest of India.

Additionally, the political leaders of these hill-communities believed, with some justification, that the British had promised them independence when they left India, as had senior Congress leaders prior to Independence. There is thus a real need for the Government of India and its organs to present a benign face to the local inhabitants, particularly in view of the Chinese claim to Arunachal Pradesh and its longer-term designs on the rest of India's north-east. The MHA, with its intimate involvement with internal security matters, should concentrate its efforts to keeping the internal security situation stable in the least forceful manner possible. Development efforts and all socio-economic as well as political measures should be progressed on priority. With enough to do on its hands, the MHA should transfer the responsibility for the Indo-Myanmar border to the MoD. The appropriate BGF for the responsibility has already been nominated and is physically wherever it needs to be. The proper solution merely requires transfer of control of the AR to the MoD, since both its two primary roles, those of border security and of COIN operations, are carried out under Army command even as per existing arrangements.

The AR are an important BGF and COIN force nominated for the security of the Indo-Myanmar border and organised for acting against UG militancy in the region. As the penultimate enforcing arm of the Indian government in the north-eastern hills and mountains, to be used only when the internal security situation cannot be brought under control by the State armed police and the CRPF, it is a very visible and important face of the Central government. Since it is tasked with use of force against Indian citizens in COIN operations, it needs to be psychologically "friends of the hill people" as much as possible, and to be able to win over their hearts and minds. It is recommended that the possibility be examined of the AR converting its class composition to a predominantly "all-Himalayan" character, with Gorkhas, Sikkimese, Monpas from Kameng in Arunachal Pradesh, Kumaonis, Garhwalis and Dogras, retaining the provision for 10 percent "locals", i.e. Assamese, Meiteis, and the various hill-communities from the mountainous and hilly regions south of the Brahmaputra valley.[7] Two problems may confront such a proposal: first, the "Annual Recruitable Male Population" estimate, based on the latest census figures, may not allow the entire AR to be manned from the Himalayan states, and second, it may not be politically expedient to increase Indian recruitment of Gorkhas from Nepal beyond existing levels.[8] A partial alternative to the predominantly "all-Himalayan" class composition could be the making up of the shortfall by enlisting suitable Adivasi soldiers from the Chhotanagpur and central Indian regions, i.e. from the Santhal, Oraon, Munda, Khadia, Maria and Gond communities, as presently make up part of the class composition of the Army's Bihar Regiment.

## Integration of Citizen-Soldiers and Reserves into the Border Defence Plan

The Army's responsibility for fighting and winning a defensive battle to protect Indian territory, without loss of territory, imposes an operational dilemma.

Fighting a defensive battle well forward, and with a linear defensive layout in the plains, means a requirement for expensive combat manpower, both for the forward battle and for successive rearward tiers of reserves. If it is possible to organise a fighting force of part-time soldiers, such as the present TA, into a combat-ready defensive force, it would reduce the pressure on the Regular Army to find enough troops. If such a re-organised TA is tasked only for its region or home state, it could be made to deploy very quickly. This distinct possibility needs to be carefully considered. TA recruitment and manning policies would need to be re-framed to suit the suggested new model.

Such a "combatised TA" model would also be eminently suitable for the coastal states, where there is very limited or practically no availability of regular Army troops in many areas. Units and formations of the suggested new form of TA, would provide a military defensive backup to the entire peninsular Indian coastline, which is inadequately catered for at present.

Additionally, while a "Cold Start" policy could take care of the requirement of extreme urgency for full-scale forward deployment, as well as of a pro-active "offensive defence" strategy, it does not address the operational scenario of a long war that remains mired in the border zone. Nor does the "fully-combatised TA" suggestion mooted above. The only truly effective answer for such a possibility is the availability of Reserve formations, i.e. Reserve infantry companies grouped into battalions, these grouped into brigades, and these in turn grouped into divisions, supported by Reserve supporting arms and services, as in regular army formations. However, such Reserve formations, and their subordinate units (e.g. battalions) could be differentiated into two or more "Readiness Levels", depending upon their state of manning, arms and equipment held, and training status. The nuclear-threat status of any war involving India and Pakistan, or India and China, or all three countries at the same time, imposes a requirement of many more medical units than in a purely conventional threat scenario, to give just one example. The possibility of creating fully-equipped non-TA Reserve medical, and communications and logistical units, to name just three possible requirements, needs to be seriously examined. Non-TA Reserve personnel would not come under the present TA system, whereby most TA personnel remain mobilised for eight to ten months of the year. Instead, such Reserve personnel, both officers and PBOR, would train perhaps twice a year for two relatively short spells, under new laws that would need to be passed for the protection of their civilian jobs.

The possibility of creating the earlier form of Army Reserve again, by induction of Army personnel on retirement into the suggested re-organised TA, also needs to be considered. In other words, the former system of "Colour Service" and "Reserve Service" needs to be re-examined for a modified applicability to the suggested new models, *provided* it is made possible to absorb Reservists into the reformed TA system. The proposed new "combatised TA" could thus in a way become a "TA-cum-Reserve".

Should a "combatised TA" become feasible, the present tasking of TA infantry battalions, that of guarding VAs and VPs in the rear of the tactical battle area, and in less threatened sectors, could easily be transferred to an enlarged and somewhat transformed Defence Security Corps (DSC). The DSC can get its manpower by transfers of serving soldiers with a certain number of years' service from all arms and services of the Army, and can be re-organised into battalions.

If it is possible to create and maintain such forces, they would need to be used in conjunction with the regular forces. All major countries which have grappled with this problem have devised some such system, as has been seen. The US, to reiterate an example, has an "all-volunteer force" combination of regular professional armed forces and a supplementary system of an Army Reserve under the federal government, which includes various technical specialists, such as doctors, and also a combatant National Guard jointly organised by the states and the federal government. The National Guard consists of fully equipped infantry, armour and artillery brigades. The entire armed forces function as a coordinated whole as a "total-force" mix of active, reserve and National Guard units. The PRC, which has conscription instead of volunteer soldiers, has the ground element of the PLA as the main force tasked for external defence, which includes its own fully-equipped reserve units and formations, supported by a fully-organised para-military Militia, whose primary mission is also external defence. The PLA is also supported by the People's Armed Police (PAP) whose primary mission is internal security, but whose secondary mission is external defence. The PAP routinely also acts as a BGF by deploying "border defence regiments". India will need to develop its own model of integration, both organisationally and for tactical military operations.

The fundamental change being suggested would be that the TA would become an active war-fighting force, using predominantly local troops fighting as part of the first line of defence against any foreign enemy ingress. TA combat units, or specialist sub-units, and where applicable, TA formation headquarters, would operate within the existing Army chain of command. One possible model is a predominantly-TA "forward brigade" which could include one regular infantry battalion, forming part of the "Order of Battle" (ORBAT) of the concerned holding division. Other TA elements could be forward-located sub-units of armour, artillery and signals. It is not impossible to have TA armoured squadrons and field artillery batteries that are equipped, practised and ready for their pre-designated defensive positions.[9] Older or obsolescent tanks and artillery could be usefully retained in service for TA units and formations. It is also possible to induct some particularly suitable artillery, even of older design, into this suggested force-mix. One such is considered particularly suitable for the "combatised TA". The old US M-114 155 mm howitzer,[10] is a towed, 155/23 design, crew-served artillery piece; a large gun system that is relatively light (5,800 kgs travelling weight) and which can be easily used for direct fire missions over open sights. The basic requirement for such a large-bore, short-barrel gun (23 calibre) is to fire High Explosive (HE) and Illuminating shells of standard 155 mm specifications, which are readily available. Guns such as this one can be freshly manufactured for India's border defence purposes in the quantities required.

The suggested Reserve part of the new TA could also provide, for example, an Armoured Delivery Regiment each for the Punjab and Rajasthan sectors, composed of former serving soldiers from the Armoured Corps. Other Reservists could hold key appointments in TA units and sub-units, where their experience from their previous Regular Army would be of great value. Actual defence of one's own homeland can be a powerful incentive to fight, if the right arms, equipment, training and organisation can be arranged. The suggested modifications and organisational methods can help harness the sentiment. Other possible alternate models of border defence by local defensive forces in conjunction with regular "main force" Army formations could also be devised. However, an evolutionary change into a finalised new system of arrangements and tactical methods would be least disruptive.

## NOTES

1. See, for example, the extensive and detailed coverage of India's military options that occupied both the print and the audio-visual media after the attack on Parliament, and during India's resultant "Operation Parakram". Media coverage named the major Indian Army formations with their locations, and debated options such as, for example, "Operation Salami Slice" and "Operation PoK Chop". See *India*

*Today*, 27 May 2002, pp. 27-34; *India Today*, 03 June 2002, pp. 23-8; *Outlook*, 03 June 2002, pp. 38-46; *India Today*, 10 June 2002, pp. 23-41; *Frontline*, 21 June 2002, pp. 4-24; and *India Today*, 23 December 2002, pp. 25-32.

2. Preface to the 22nd Report of the Standing Committee on Defence (2006-2007), 14th Lok Sabha, July 2007, pp. v-vi.
3. This is unfortunate in that the BGF actions are anti-foreigner, and based on existing Indian laws, rather than anti-Muslim.
4. As recommended by Lt Gen Arvind Sharma, PVSM, AVSM, VSM (Retd), former GOC-in-C Eastern Command, and former GOC 14 Corps, during an interview with this author on 02 May 2009.
5. As per Arun Shourie, MP, Rajya Sabha, in the 14th and 15th Lok Sabha, and Member, Parliamentary Standing Committee on Defence, during his lecture on "India's National Security," at the United Service Institution of India, on 29 April 2009.
6. Under Jehangir, the Mughal Empire had tried to annex Assam from 1615 onwards. Though the Ahoms were defeated in the first Mughal-Ahom battle in 1615, the Mughals were unable to consolidate their hold due to the Ahoms continuing with guerrilla warfare. Under Aurangzeb's directions, a second campaign was launched by the Mughal Subahdar of Bengal, Mir Jumla, from 1660 onwards, and again the Ahoms were defeated in battle in 1661, but continued to fight till the decisive Battle of Saraighat (in the Guwahati area) in December 1667. This was fought between a much-larger Mughal army led by the Kacchwaha Rajput king Raja Ramsingh and the Ahom kingdom under their king Lachit Borphukan. The Mughal army was comprehensively defeated by the Ahoms' brilliant use of terrain, guerrilla tactics, psychological warfare and military intelligence, and since 1682, Assam had remained politically distinct from India.
7. British supremacy over the entire area was maintained in the early years by the use of force when necessary, using battalions of Gorkha infantry raised for the purpose. These units were the direct linear ancestors of the first few battalions of the AR, and the first two battalions of the Army's regiment "The 8th Gorkha Rifles", which was then based in Shillong, and which for many years, carried the sub-title 'The Assam Regiment". (It had no connection with today's Assam Regiment, which is composed of soldiers from all the northeastern States. This regiment was raised during the Second World War.) The first four battalions of today's AR have origins starting from 1835, and were formally designated battalions in 1870. These constituted the punitive military force for keeping this eastern buffer zone under control. This eastern buffer zone system was duplicated later in the north-west, where the British created another buffer zone. Here they sought to insulate the Punjab from the Pathan tribes of Afghanistan. They thus annexed part of Pathan territory under a forced 1893 agreement with Afghanistan for British control up to the Durand Line. This buffer zone was named the North-West Frontier Province, and a punitive military force named the Punjab Frontier Force was created. Its direct linear descendants exist today in the Pakistan Army, such as the Frontier Force (FF) Regiment, with an infantry regiment in the Indian Army, viz. the 5th Gorkha Rifles (Frontier Force), and a few batteries in some artillery regiments.

8. Recruitment of Gorkhas of Indian domicile and nationality poses no problem other than that of availability of suitable volunteer human material.
9. Author's discussion with Maj Gen KVS Lalotra, AVSM, YSM, SM, Additional Director-General TA, on 05 May 2009.
10. The US M-114 howitzer fires a 43 kg HE shell to a maximum range of 14 kms, can fire 2 rounds in the first 30 seconds of going into action, 8 rounds in the first 4 minutes, has a burst rate of fire of 4 rounds per minute, and a sustained rate of fire of 40 rounds per hour.

# APPENDICES

APPENDIX I

# Border Area Development Programme

The Border Area Development Programme (BADP) is part of the comprehensive approach to the Border Management with focus on socio-economic development of the border areas and to promote a sense of security amongst the people living there. The programme was started during the 7$^{th}$ Plan with the objective of balanced development of sensitive border areas in the western region through adequate provision of infrastructural facilities. The programme has been subsequently extended to States bordering Bangladesh, Myanmar, China, Bhutan and Nepal and it now covers 358 border blocks of 94 districts of seventeen (17) States, which share international land border with neighboring countries.

BADP is a 100% centrally funded programme. The main objective of the programme is to meet the special developmental needs of the people living in remote and inaccessible areas situated near the International Border. The schemes/works like construction/maintenance of roads, water supply, education, sports, filling gaps in infrastructure, security, organisation of early childhood care and education centre, education for physically handicapped and backward Sections etc. are being undertaken under the BADP. Preference is given to the villages/habitations which are closer to the border line.

## Guidelines of BADP

The Border Area Development Programme (BADP) is implemented under the guidelines framed by the Planning Commission. The funds are allocated by the Planning Commission annually which are re-allocated to the Border States taking into consideration (i) length of International Border (km); (ii) Population of the border block and (iii) Area of the border block (sq. km). Weightage of 15% over and above the total allocation is also given to States having hilly/desert/kuchchh areas. The funds are additive to normal Central assistance and are allocated for addressing the special problems faced by the people of the border areas.

Schemes/works to be undertaken under BADP are finalised and approved by the State Level Screening Committee (SLSC) headed by the Chief Secretary of the concerned State and executed by the agencies of the State Government. Security related schemes can be taken up under BADP but the expenditure on such schemes should not exceed 10% of the total allocation in a particular year. The funds under BADP are to be used for schemes in the identified border blocks only.

## Monitoring Mechanisms and Review of BADP Works

Implementation of BADP, in terms of physical and financial achievements, is being monitored regularly in the Department of Border Management. The State Governments are also closely monitoring the implementation of works/ schemes being undertaken under BADP. The inspection of the works is also being carried out by the officers of the Department of Border Management to ensure quality and timely completion of the works.

## Empowered Committee

An Empowered Committee under the chairmanship of Secretary, Border Management has been constituted to examine various aspects relating to scope of the Programme, its execution, prescription of geographical limits, allocation of funds etc. Setting up of Micro Hydel Projects (MHPs) in J&K An amount of Rs.532.25 lakh has been released to Government of J&K during 2004-05 and 2005-06 for installation of Micro Hydel Projects (MHPs) through Army in the remote border areas. The work is under progress.

## Optimal Utilisation of Waters of Eastern Rivers of Indus River System

Given the importance of Optimal Utilisation of Waters of the Eastern Rivers of Indus River System, it has been taken up under the Border Area Development Programme (BADP) in States of Punjab (03 projects) and Jammu & Kashmir (06 projects) as a special initiative. An amount of Rs.3023.50 lakh (Punjab—Rs.1994.00 lakh and J&K—Rs.1029.50 lakh) has been released during the year 2005-06 and 2006-07. Work on two projects (Madhopur and Hussainiwala headworks) in Punjab has been completed and work on third project (Harike headwork) is under progress whereas work on the projects in J&K is going on. Rs.25.00 crore has been earmarked for this purpose for J&K during 2007-08.

## Special Initiative

Special initiative has been taken on development of social and economic infrastructure, promotion of people's participation in development, elimination of sense of alienation and insecurity from minds of the people so as to create conditions conducive to social and economic progress. An amount of Rs.13007.31 lakh has been released to States during 2007-08 for this purpose and State Schemes/Cluster Approach which could be implemented in a time frame of 1-2 years. Some of the areas suggested to the States are:

(i) **Model Village:** Composite development of at least one village of sizeable population surrounded by five-six or more villages close to the border area block as Model village.

(ii) **Health:** Mobile dispensary fitted with necessary portable equipment.

(iii) **Livelihood:** Community-based infrastructure like forestry, pasture land, sheds for livestock (only for BPL), floriculture park, fishery ponds, multi-utility community centres, mini hat Mini marketing yards, herbal, medicinal and aromatic parks.

(iv) **Power:** Solar and mini-hydel projects, bio-gas-mass gasification and wind energy.

(v) **Tourism and Sports:** Sports facilities, tourism/adventure tourism facilities like canteen parking, public conveniences.

## Task Force on BADP

In a meeting held in July, 2005 in Prime Minister's Office, it was decided to set up Task Force for reorientation of Border Area Development Programme. The Task Force was accordingly constituted under the Chairmanship of Shri B.N. Yugandhar, Member Planning Commission in October, 2005. The Task Force has submitted its Report in July, 2007.

## Allocation and Releases

An amount of Rs.52000 lakh has been allocated for BADP for the year 2007-08 which is at par to the previous year's allocation. Allocation and releases made to the Border States during the financial years 2006-07 and 2007-08 are as under:

| Sl. No. | Name of States | 2006-07 | | 2007-08 | |
|---|---|---|---|---|---|
| | | Final Allocation | Release | Allocation | Release |
| 1. | Arunachal Pradesh | 4498.00 | 4498.00 | 4733.00 | 4577.52 |
| 2. | Assam | 2338.34 | 2338.34 | 2017.00 | 1344.67 |
| 3. | Bihar | 3119.00 | 3119.00 | 3172.00 | 3172.00 |
| 4. | Gujarat | 2096.00 | 2096.00 | 2420.00 | 1344.65 |
| 5. | Himachal Pradesh | 1269.00 | 1269.00 | 1119.00 | 746.00 |
| 6. | Jammu & Kashmir | 9793.05 | 9793.05 | 7483.00 | 4569.67 |
| 7. | Manipur | 1250.00 | 1250.00 | 1121.00 | 738.74 |
| 8. | Meghalaya | 1313.36 | 1313.36 | 1029.00 | 686.00 |
| 9. | Mizoram | 2262.00 | 2262.00 | 2086.00 | 2086.00 |
| 10. | Nagaland | 1577.00 | 1577.00 | 1000.00 | 666.67 |
| 11. | Punjab | 3641.12 | 3641.12 | 1870.00 | 1870.00 |
| 12. | Rajasthan | 5731.36 | 5731.36 | 7659.00 | 7652.00 |
| 13. | Sikkim | 1566.04 | 1566.04 | 1000.00 | 636.67 |
| 14. | Tripura | 2678.48 | 2678.48 | 2287.00 | 1510.31 |
| 15. | Uttar Pradesh | 2231.00 | 2231.00 | 2473.00 | 1348.81 |
| 16. | Uttarakhand | 871.00 | 871.00 | 1895.00 | - |
| 17. | West Bengal | 5765.25 | 5765.25 | 7992.00 | 4194.05 |
| | Total | 52000.00 | 52000.00 | 51356.00 + 644.00* | 37143.76 |

*Kept reserved for contingencies etc.

Annexure-I

**Ministry of Home Affairs**
**Department of Border Management**
**Border Area Develoment Programme(BADP)**

Statement showing the allocation, release and expenditure during the year 2004-05 to 2007-08

**Position as on 13.02.2008**
(*Rs in lakh*)

| States | 2004-05 | | | 2005-06 | | | 2006-07 | | | 2007-08 | |
|---|---|---|---|---|---|---|---|---|---|---|---|
| | Release | Expenditure | Unspent Balance | Release | Expenditure | Unspent Balance | Release | Expenditure | Unspent Balance | Allocation | Release |
| Arunachal Pradesh | 1351.00 | 1351.00 | NIL | 1935.49 | 1925.00 | 10.49 | 4498.00 | 388.13 | 4109.87 | 4733.00 | 4577.52 |
| Assam | 998.00 | 998.00 | NIL | 1081.00 | 1009.57 | 71.43 | 2338.34 | 551.73 | 1786.61 | 2017.00 | 1945.57 |
| Bihar | 728.00 | 728.00 | NIL | 1693.00 | 1693.00 | NIL | 3119.00 | 2043.61 | 1075.39 | 3172.00 | 3172.00 |
| Gujrat | 1313.06 | 1313.06 | NIL | 1106.00 | 935.72 | 170.28 | 2096.00 | 518.08 | 1577.92 | 2420.00 | 2249.72 |
| Himachal Pradesh | 1148.96 | 1148.96 | NIL | 642.05 | 642.05 | NIL | 1269.00 | 178.90 | 1090.10 | 1119.00 | 1119.00 |
| Jammu & Kashmir | 8695.00 | 8695.00 | NIL | 9999.97 | 9999.97 | NIL | 9793.05 | 8985.61 | 807.44 | 4983.00 | 4983.00 |
| J&K Indus Water projects/strategic roads | - | - | - | - | - | - | - | - | - | 2500.00 | 2500.00 |
| Manipur$ | 555.00 | 555.00 | NIL | 592.00 | 583.41 | 8.59 | 1250.00 | 903.73 | 346.27 | 1121.00 | 1112.41 |
| Meghalaya | 900.00 | 900.00 | NIL | 494.00 | 494.00 | NIL | 1313.36 | 1313.36 | Nil | 1029.00 | 1029.00 |
| Mizoram | 1556.00 | 1556.00 | NIL | 903.48 | 903.48 | NIL | 2262.00 | 1270.17 | 991.83 | 2086.00 | 2086.00 |
| Nagaland | 416.00 | 416.00 | NIL | 456.00 | 456.00 | NIL | 1577.00 | 478.00 | 1099.00 | 1000.00 | 1000.00 |
| Punjab | 992.51 | 992.51 | NIL | 1308.00 | 1308.00 | NIL | 3641.12 | 1277.36 | 2363.76 | 1870.00 | 1870.00 |
| Rajasthan | 3695.29 | 3695.29 | NIL | 3835.00 | 3835.00 | NIL | 5731.36 | 0.00 | 5731.36 | 7659.00 | 7659.00 |
| Sikkim | 1256.20 | 1256.20 | NIL | 622.00 | 622.00 | NIL | 1566.04 | 293.30 | 1272.74 | 1000.00 | 940.00 |
| Tripura | 2109.60 | 2105.49 | 4.11 | 1296.00 | 1296.00 | NIL | 2678.48 | 925.53 | 1752.95 | 2287.00 | 2282.89 |
| Uttar Pradesh | 1654.70 | 1654.70 | NIL | 1399.01 | 1099.56 | 299.45 | 2231.00 | 193.37 | 2037.63 | 2473.00 | 2173.55 |
| Uttarakhand | 1389.94 | 835.79 | 554.15 | 977.00 | 827.97 | 149.03 | 871.00 | 160.33 | 710.67 | 1895.00 | 512.49 |
| West Bengal | 3739.95 | 3367.00 | 372.95 | 4160.00 | 3536.00 | 624.00 | 5765.25 | 3116.00 | 2649.25 | 7992.00 | 6880.05 |
| Total | 32499.21 | 31568.00 | 931.21 | 32500.00 | 31166.73 | 1333.27 | 52000.00 | 22597.21 | 29402.79 | 51356.00 | 48092.20 |
| | | | | | | Kept Reserved for contingencies etc. | | | | 644.00 | |
| | | | | | | | Grant Total | | | 52000.00 | |

APPENDIX II

# Coastal Security Scheme

A Coastal Security Scheme has been formulated for strengthening infrastructure for patrolling and surveillance of country's coastal areas, particularly the shallow areas close to coast to check and counter illegal cross border activities and criminal activities using coast or sea. The scheme is being implemented in all the 9 coastal States and 4 Union Territories from the year 2005-06. Under the scheme, assistance is been given to the coastal States and Union Territories to set up 73 coastal police stations which will be equipped with 204 boats, 153 jeeps and 312 motor cycles for mobility on coast and in close coastal waters. The costal police stations will also have a marine police with personnel trained in maritime activities. A lumpsum assistance of Rs.10 lakh per police station will also be given for equipment, computer, furniture etc. Assistance will be given to the States and UTs to meet the cost of fuel, maintenance and repairs of the boats for 5 years. Statewise details of the components of assistance under the scheme are given below :

| Sl. No. | Name of the State/ UT | Coastal Police Stations | Vessels | Jeeps | Motor Cycles | Check Posts | Out Posts | Barracks | Other items | Approved Outlay (Rs. in lakhs) |
|---|---|---|---|---|---|---|---|---|---|---|
| 1 | Gujarat | 10 | 30 | 20 | 101 | 25 | 46 | - | - | 5842.60 |
| 2 | Maharashtra | 12 | 28 | 25 | 57 | 32 | - | 24 | - | 4092.60 |
| 3 | Goa | 3 | 9 | 6 | 9 | - | - | - | RIB-10 | 1653.50 |
| 4 | Karnataka | 5 | 15 | 9 | 4 | - | - | - | - | 2711.90 |
| 5 | Kerala | 8 | 24 | 16 | 24 | - | - | - | - | 4356.00 |
| 6 | Tamilnadu | 12 | 24 | 12 | 36 | 40 | 12 | - | - | 4408.00 |
| 7 | Andhra Pradesh | 6 | 18 | 12 | 18 | - | - | - | - | 3267.00 |
| 8 | Orissa | 5 | 15 | 10 | 15 | - | - | - | - | 2722.50 |
| 9 | West Bengal | 6 | 18 | 12 | 12 | - | - | 6 | - | 3353.40 |
| 10 | Pondicherry | 1 | 3 | 2 | 3 | - | - | - | - | 544.50 |

*Contd.*

| Sl. No. | Name of the State/ UT | Coastal Police Stations | Vessels | Jeeps | Motor Cycles | Check Posts | Out Posts | Barracks | Other items | Approved Outlay (Rs. in lakhs) |
|---|---|---|---|---|---|---|---|---|---|---|
| 11 | Lakkshadweep | 4 | 6 | 8 | 8 | - | - | - | - | 936.80 |
| 12 | Daman & Diu | 1 | 4 | 3 | 5 | - | - | - | - | 668.35 |
| 13 | A&N Islands | - | 10 | 18 | 20 | - | - | - | - | 2604.00 |
| | Total | 73 | 204 | 153 | 312 | 97 | 58 | 30 | 10 | 37161.15 |

## Progress of Implementation

47 out of 73 coastal police stations proposed have been made operational in Gujarat (10), Andhra Pradesh (6), West Bengal (4), Goa (3), Kerala (1), Maharashtra (12), Karnataka (5), Puduchery (1), Lakshadweep (4) and Daman & Diu (1).

Boats are being procured centrally for which M/s Goa Shipyards Limited, Goa and M/s Garden Reach Ship Builders and Engineers Limited, Kolkata have been nominated. Delivery of the boats is scheduled to commence in the 13th month after signing of the agreement with suppliers.

Coast Guard is imparting training to the State Police personnel in maritime activities. The training is being imparted in the District Headquarters of the Coast Guard.

During the year 2005-06 and 2006-07, Rs.13.04 crore and Rs.11.65 crore have been released to the State Governments and Union Territories concerned as assistance under this Scheme. During 2007-08, Rs.4.09 crore have been released to the States and UTs so far.

APPENDIX III

# Fencing and Flood Lighting of Borders

Fencing and flood lighting of the border are important constituents of maintaining vigilance along the borders. In order to curb infiltration, smuggling and other anti-national activities from across Indo-Pakistan and Indo-Bangladesh borders, the Government has undertaken the work of construction of fencing, flood lighting and roads along these borders.

## (a) Indo-Bangladesh Border (IBB)

The Indian side of the Indo-Bangladesh border passes through West Bengal (2216.7 kms), Assam (263 kms), Meghalaya (443 kms), Tripura (856 kms) and Mizoram (318 kms). The entire stretch consists of plain, riverine, hilly/jungle and with hardly any natural obstacles. The area is heavily populated, and the cultivation is carried out till the last inch of the border.

The Indo-Bangladesh border is marked by a high degree of porosity and checking illegal cross border activities has been a challenging proposition. The main problem is of illegal migration from Bangladesh into India. In order to prevent illegal immigration and other anti-national activities from across the border, the Government of India had sanctioned the construction of border roads and fencing in two phases. The total length of Indo-Bangladesh border to be fenced is 3286.87 kms out of which 2535.80 kms of fencing has so far been completed. The work of construction of fencing in approximately 751 kms is under implementation. Out of this, work of construction of fencing in 296 kms in Mizoram sector, where the work started only in 2005, would be completed during the year 2007-08. Fencing has not been undertaken in remaining length on account of non-feasibility, riverine/low lying areas, population within 150 yards of the border, pending land acquisition cases. An additional length of 120 kms in Tripura, which was not originally sanctioned to be part of Phase-II, will also be taken up during the year 2007-08.

In addition, 3250.60 kms of border roads have also been constructed out of sanctioned length of 3663 kms. The phase wise progress of fencing and roads as on 31st December, 2007 is as under:

**Fencing**

*(Length in kms)*

| Name of State | Border Length | Fencing in Phase-I (completed) | Fencing in Phase-II (sanctioned) | Fencing in Phase-II (completed) | Total completed in Phase-I & II |
|---|---|---|---|---|---|
| West Bengal | 2216.7 | 507 | 1021 | 674.05 | 1181.05 |
| Assam | 263 | 149.29 | 71.5 | 51.42 | 200.71 |
| Meghalaya | 443 | 198.06 | 201 | 180.19 | 378.25 |
| Tripura | 856 | - | 736 | 668.04 | 668.04 |
| Mizoram | 318 | - | 400 | 107.75 | 107.75 |
| Total | 4096.7 | 854.35 | 2429.5 | 1681.45 | 2535.80 |

**Border Roads**

*(Length in kms)*

| Name of State | Roads in Phase-I (completed) | Roads in Phase-II (sanctioned) | Roads in Phase-II (completed) | Total (completed) |
|---|---|---|---|---|
| West Bengal | 1616.57 | — | — | 1616.57 |
| Assam | 176.50 | 77.50 | 61.70 | 238.20 |
| Meghalaya | 211.29 | 204 | 200.85 | 412.14 |
| Tripura | 480.51 | 269 | 210.14 | 690.65 |
| Mizoram | 153.06 | 246.50 | 139.98 | 293.04 |
| Total | 2637.93 | 797.00 | 612.67 | 3250.60 |

277 kms of floodlighting has been completed in West Bengal as a pilot project. The Government has decided to undertake floodlighting in 2840 kms along the entire length of Indo-Bangladesh border, in the stretches where the fencing has been erected, at an estimate cost of Rs.1327.00 crore. The floodlighting works are expected to commence during the year 2007-08 and would be completed by the year 2011-12.

*Replacement of fencing constructed under Phase-I*

The Government of India has decided to replace the entire 861 kms of fence constructed under Phase-I in West Bengal, Assam and Meghalaya, as most of this fence has been damaged due to adverse climatic conditions, repeated submergence etc. The replacement work has already commenced in the States of Assam and West Bengal. 193.70 kms of fencing has been replaced so far.

### (b) Indo-Pakistan Border

India shares 3323 kms (including Line of Control (LoC) in Jammu & Kashmir sector) of its land border with Pakistan. This border runs along the States of Gujarat, Rajasthan, Punjab and Jammu & Kashmir. The Indo-Pakistan border has varied terrain and distinct geographical features. This border is characterised by attempts at infiltration by terrorists and smuggling of arms, ammunition and contraband, the Line of Control being the most active and live portion of the border.

*Punjab and Rajasthan*

A total length of 462.45 kms and 461 kms has been fenced and flood lit respectively in the entire Punjab sector, except some gaps in riverine areas. In Rajasthan sector also, the work of construction of fencing and flood lighting in 1048 kms and 1023 kms respectively has been completed except certain shifting sand dune areas.

*Jammu*

In Jammu sector, the work of construction of 185 kms of fencing has been completed. 175.50 kms of floodlighting works have also been completed and work on 9.96 kms will be undertaken after realignment of fencing. Work of floodlighting in a length of 0.54 kms is in progress.

*Gujarat*

With the sealing of Punjab and Rajsthan borders, vulnerability of Gujarat border to infiltration and other illegal cross-border activities has increased. Therefore, the Government approved a comprehensive proposal for erecting fencing, flood lighting and construction of border/link roads and Border Out-Posts for Border Security Force in the Gujarat sector of the Indo-Pak border. So far, 217 kms of fencing and 202 kms of flood lighting have been completed in the Gujarat sector out of 310 kms sanctioned.

There has been time overrun in completing the project due to unforeseen circumstances and natural calamities including devastating earthquake in 2001, unprecedented rains and consequential floods in 2003 and 2006. The cost of the project has also increased considerably due to price escalation, increase in the scope of work, upgradation of specifications for roads and electrical works etc. In addition, an expenditure of Rs.223.00 crore is estimated for upgradation works as per Central Road Research Institute (CRRI) recommendations after floods in 2006. Approval of the Cabinet Committee on Security for extension of time for completion of fencing/floodlighting project in Gujarat sector and revised cost is being obtained.

The status of progress of fencing and floodlighting on the Indo-Pak border as on 31st December, 2007 is as under:

**Fencing** *(Length in kms)*

| Name of the State | Total length of border | Total length of border to be fenced | Length of the border fenced so far | Remaining length of the border proposed to be fenced |
|---|---|---|---|---|
| Punjab | 553 | 461 | 462.45* | - |
| Rajasthan | 1037 | 1056.63 | 1048.27* | - |
| Jammu International Border | 210 | 186 | 185 | 1 |
| Gujarat | 508 | 310 | 217 | 93 |
| Total | 2308 | 2007.63 | 1912.72 | 94 |

*Length is more due to topographical factors/alignment of fencing.

**Floodlighting** *(Length in kms)*

| Name of the State | Total length of border | Total length of border to be floodlit | Length of the border floodlit so far | Remaining length of the border proposed to be floodlit |
|---|---|---|---|---|
| Punjab | 553 | 460.72 | 460.72 | - |
| Rajasthan | 1037 | 1022.80 | 1022.80 | - |
| Jammu International Border | 210 | 186 | 175.50 | 10.50 |
| Gujarat | 508 | 310 | 202 | 108 |
| Total | 2308 | 1979.52 | 1861.02 | 118.50 |

### *Proposal for Shifting of Fencing Close to the Border*

#### *Jammu IB*

Initially, due to heavy fire from across the border, in a stretch of 38.015 kms IPB fence was erected at a distance, varying from 400 meters to 1.5 kms away from the IB. After the ceasefire, there were representations from the border inhabitants, political parties and others to shift the fence closer to the IB.

The matter was accordingly examined and it was decided to shift 38.015 kms of fencing erected on Jammu International Border close to the border to facilitate the border inhabitants to cultivate their lands without problems. The estimated cost of the proposed shifting of fence will be Rs.28.34 crore. The work of shifting the fence will be undertaken during the year 2007-08.

*Punjab*

BSF has proposed shifting of 23.380 kms of fencing closer to the border in certain stretches of Ferozepur sector in Punjab due to the problems being faced by the farmers in cultivating their lands. Cost estimates of the proposal are being worked out by CPWD. The work is expected to commence during 2007-08.

# Index

## U



## V



## W